# The Fantastic in Literature

## by Eric S. Rabkin

PRINCETON UNIVERSITY PRESS

PRINCETON, NEW JERSEY

Library of Congress Cataloging in Publication Data
will be found on the last printed page of this book

Publication of this book has been aided by a grant from
The Andrew W. Mellon Foundation

This book has been composed in Linotype Janson

Printed in the United States of America
by Princeton University Press
Princeton, New Jersey

Second hardcover printing, with corrections, 1977

First PRINCETON PAPERBACK printing, 1977

# The Fantastic in Literature

# Contents

vii

# Preface

*The Fantastic in Literature* explores the nature and uses of
the fantastic. By examining what makes Fantasy special, we
can isolate the affect (in the psychological sense of the
noun) that flavors so much of our experience of art. This
book attempts to explore the mechanisms that generate that
affect, following their trail into the worlds of fairy tale,
science fiction, detective fiction, religious allegory, and so
on, finally reaching the wider field of human psychology.
The theoretical positions that emerge in this enterprise have
methodological consequences that I believe open up new
avenues for the study of worldview, genre criticism, and literary history. This book, then, treats not only Fantasy, but
the fantastic; it deals not only in the concrete but in the
theoretical. In order that the examples used here might interilluminate, they are drawn primarily from one cultural
moment, in this case England of the late Victorian era.
However, in each part of the argument, this limit of con-
venience is widened in ways that I hope will imply the gen-
erality of the theoretical conclusions. For example, in discussing the phenomenon of Gothicism as an example of
literary history, the temporal limit is expanded to include
works written between 1700 and the present; in studying
the genre of science fiction, the national limit is extended to
include American works (as well as some Continental examples); and in discussing such general notions as "escape,"
the limits of time and nation are removed entirely. While
focusing on a single time and place for argumentative economy, I have attempted a treatment throughout that acknowl-

edges that the subject of this book is as large as the unend-
ing stream of imaginings that flows from the human mind.

In pursuing the fantastic, I have been much helped. I am
happy to thank my students at the University of Michigan,
whose questions and suggestions molded my preliminary
thinking. My own research at the British Museum was
made possible by the kindness of the Horace H. Rackham
School of Graduate Study of the University of Michigan,
which awarded me a travel grant, and by the American
Council of Learned Societies, whose Fellowship in 1973 allowed me essential time to digest that research and refine
my conclusions. And, I must try to express my thanks to
Elizabeth Jane Rabkin, my patient, thoughtful wife, who
helped me in all ways, and helps me always.

# Bibliographic Note

MANY of the works cited in this volume, such as popular novels, do not exist in standard library editions. Where that is the case, the citations are to the most widely available current editions.

The Fantastic in Literature

*"Well, now that we have seen each other,"*
*said the Unicorn, "if you'll believe in me,*
*I'll believe in you. Is that a bargain?"*

—Lewis Carroll

# ❦ I ❧

# The Fantastic and Fantasy

*"Oh Tiger-lily!" said Alice, addressing herself to one*
*that was waving gracefully about in the wind, "I wish you*
*could talk!"*
*"We can talk," said the Tiger-lily, "when there's any-*
*body worth talking to."*
*Alice was so astonished that she couldn't speak for a*
*minute: it quite seemed to take her breath away.*

—LEWIS CARROLL[1]

WHAT exactly is the fantastic? In the twentieth-century
world, our preconceptions of the impossible are assaulted
every day. Some men learn computer-assisted porpoise language while others shriek at baboons; gentle people all over
the world spend hours thinking well of their houseplants.
In a context combining these points of view, one could believe a report of the creation of a device that allowed people and plants to communicate. According to the conventions of such early telepathy novels as A. E. van Vogt's *Slan*
(1940), people/plant communication would be more a
"cluster of emotions, an uncontrollable influx" than it would
be formal logical discourse, but what of that? Alice might
have been astonished at talking plants, but we moderns can
see such phenomena as perfectly orderly, as unexpected but

[1] Lewis Carroll, *Through the Looking Glass*, in *The Annotated
Alice*, Martin Gardner, ed., World Publishing Company, New
York, 1960, p. 200. This volume also contains *Alice's Adventures in
Wonderland*. Because Mr. Gardner's scholarship is invaluable, and
because his text is available and authoritative, all references to these
two Alice books are to his edition.

3

nicely complementary data in the notebook of the world's experience. Talking plants—and (Komodo) dragons for that matter—are not inherently fantastic; they become so when seen from a certain perspective. The fantastic does more than extend experience; the fantastic contradicts perspectives. Alice's astonishment signals the fantastic.

It is perfectly conceivable, if not today then a century hence,[2] that normative, shared reality, the set of perspectives that gets one through physical transactions like obtaining food and moving one's body from place to place, may well include the view that plants can talk. But in that future century, *Through the Looking Glass* will still be a fantasy. When Alice says " 'I *wish* you could talk!' " the implied author behind the text is reminding us today that flowers are preconceived as mute; in future times, that same line may merely remind readers that in 1872, when the book was published, people once saw plants as mute. Those future readers willing to suspend their disbelief in mute plants will be rewarded by a delightful fantasy. Those who aren't willing to follow the signs in the text will throw down the book in distaste. Unless one participates sympathetically in the ground rules of a narrative world, no occurrence in that world can make sense—or even nonsense.

The ability of art to create its own interior set of ground rules is fundamental to the aesthetic experience, an ability that Tolkien calls "subcreation,"[3] but which more generally falls under the term "decorum." Every work of art sets up its own ground rules. The perspectives that the fantastic

---

[2] "A Century Hence" is the title of a utopian vision (1880) in undistinguished verse that closely presages the more thoughtful work of Edward Bellamy. Paxton's poem is available in *SF: The Other Side of Realism*, Thomas D. Clareson, ed., Bowling Green University Popular Press, Bowling Green, Ohio, 1971, pp. 282-287.

[3] J.R.R. Tolkien, "On Fairy Stories," in *The Tolkien Reader*, Ballantine, New York, 1966, p. 47.

contradicts are perspectives legitimized by these internal ground rules. Alice's underscored *wish* performs such a legitimization, and, coming immediately before the flower's answer, would always perform such a legitimization, whether the armchair world conceived of flowers as talkative or mute.

From "a certain Chinese encyclopedia entitled *Celestial Emporium of Benevolent Knowledge*," Borges offers[4] a collection of what one might call "incommensurate categories," a collection whose strange effect on the reader emphasizes the subcreative power of words to establish a set of ground rules for the duration of the reading moment:

> On those remote pages it is written that animals are divided into (a) those that belong to the Emperor, (b) embalmed ones, (c) those that are trained, (d) suckling pigs, (e) mermaids, (f) fabulous ones, (g) stray dogs, (h) those that are included in this classification, (i) those that tremble as if they were mad, (j) innumerable ones, (k) those drawn with a very fine camel's hair brush, (l) others, (m) those that have just broken a flower vase, (n) those that resemble flies from a distance.

For whatever reasons, perhaps the habit of Aristotelian two-valued logic, perhaps some natural Kantian category of thought, each of these lettered classes not only identifies a group of animals, but identifies a grouping principle. These subliminal principles foist perspectives on us as readers. When the grouping principles underlying later categories contradict the perspectives subcreated by having read earlier categories, we feel the same bemused wrenching that Alice feels as *astonishment*.

4 Jorge Luis Borges, *Other Inquisitions 1937-1952*, Ruth L. C. Simms, transl., Washington Square Press, New York, 1966, p. 108.

We would expect after "(a) those that belong to the Emperor" either "those that do not" or any one of the categories in the form "those that belong to . . . ," such as "those that belong to the Empress." Of course, we get no such grouping, so we begin to perform mental acrobatics to make sense of the collection. One possible explanation for "(a)" standing alone is that *all* animals might belong to the Emperor. But then, why mention "(a)" as a "division" of the animals? This collection of groups feels fantastic in the reading; however, we read "(b)" through "(n)" as fantastic not because all animals do or don't belong to the Emperor, but because those elements of the text contradict a perspective earlier foisted on the reader by the very process of reading "(a)."

In similar fashion, one can identify numerous other contradictions: "(e) mermaids," for example, are the first "fabulous" creatures in the list; hence they question the notion that these categories contain "real" animals. But a true contradiction occurs with "(f) fabulous ones," because if this category is *different* from "(e) mermaids," then the writer of the list seems to think that mermaids are real! Fantastic. All of these little aesthetic shocks arise only because we have accepted the premise that animals are "divided into" these classes, rather than "burdened with these labels." It is reasonable, of course, to call one object dime, coin, silver, money, circle, and counter, depending on the circumstances.[5] But literature controls tightly the circumstances that come to a reader's mind, and therefore much fun can be had by capitalizing on the common epistemological error of confusing "identifying" with "labelling." We have not

[5] An excellent discussion of the relation between language acquisition and the functional structure of one's world is available in R. Brown, "How shall a thing be called?" in *Language*, R. C. Oldfield and J. C. Marshall, eds., Penguin Books, Baltimore, 1968, pp. 82-91.

identified an animal by calling it the Emperor's if all animals are the Emperor's. We've merely put a label on it. This is clear in the category of "(g) stray dogs," a category of labels alone since only the owner and the dog, and maybe not even they, can know whether any given dog wandering down any given road is stray, and thereby identify the animal as belonging to division "(g)."

Another key item in Borges' list is "(l) others." This category implies the end of the list itself, and fosters ideas not about the views of the list-maker, but about the structure of the list. When the list continues, a purely aesthetic conception is contradicted, and we receive a new fantastic shock. But note: this shock arises not from our perspectives on the nature of the animal kingdom, nor does it arise from our knowledge of what might have been believed of the animal kingdom at the time of writing the *Celestial Emporium* (if indeed Borges has not further fooled us by inventing his own encyclopedia), but our shock comes from our apprehension of the structure of the list we are in the very process of reading. We find that "(l)" plus any later grouping yields a contradiction in structure. This source of the fantastic depends not at all on the reader's perspectives on the world, but rather on the reader's willing participation in the text.

Borges' whimsy teaches us that the fantastic can exist wholly within the world of language. It does not matter whether any given readers at any given time tell themselves that flowers can or cannot talk; in reading *Through the Looking Glass* we are taught that one of the ground rules of the narrative world in which the mind is adventuring is that flowers do not talk. And when this perspective is contradicted, turned directly around, our shock is validated by Alice's reported reaction: "it quite seemed to take her breath away."

One of the key distinguishing marks of the fantastic is that the perspectives enforced by the ground rules of the narrative world must be diametrically contradicted. The reconfiguration of meanings must make an exact flip-flop, an opposition from up to down, from + to —. Lewis Carroll realized this and based his many logic jokes on such diametrical reconfigurations:

> "When you say 'hill,' " the [Red] Queen interrupted, "*I* could show you hills, in comparison with which you'd call that a valley."
>
> "No, I shouldn't," said Alice, surprised into contradicting her at last: "a hill *can't* be a valley, you know. That would be nonsense—"[6]

Precisely. By virtue of this notion of diametric reconfiguration, direct contradiction of perspectives, we can distinguish the fantastic from other non-normal occurrences: the unexpected and the irrelevant.

*Unexpected*, literally, means *not-expected*. When a hitherto unmentioned character wanders into a story, his entrance is not-expected, but may be quite ordinary. For example, in *Hard Times* (1854), Dickens' great novel of the social abuses caused by utilitarianism in England's emerging industrial cities, Stephen Blackpool, one of the main characters, is not even mentioned until chapter 10. However, his injection into the work, though not expected, is perfectly in keeping with the ground rules previously legitimized by the narrative: where Gradgrindism serves the interests of dehumanizing manufacture, there must be dehumanized workers to man the machines. In the sense of *not-expected*, unexpected occurrences have little to do with the fantastic.

More nearly allied to the fantastic is what one might call

[6] Lewis Carroll, *Through the Looking Glass*, p. 207.

the *dis-expected*, those elements which the text had diverted one from thinking about but which, it later turns out, are in perfect keeping with the ground rules of the narrative. Jokes depend on the dis-expected. Arthur Koestler[7] makes this point clear, using other terms, in his analysis of one of Freud's famous examples: A chorus girl believes the lavishness of her elderly admirer's gifts indicates too serious a yearning on his part and tries to put him off by saying, "Sir, I must tell you, my hand belongs to another." "My dear," he replies, "I never aspired that high."[8] The overt concern with formal propriety makes sexual references dis-expected; the last line with its formal rhetoric confirms the importance of propriety. However, as soon as we realize the covert implication of the roué's double entendre, we immediately make a back-formation that organizes the covert implications of *chorus girl* and *admirer*. Then, the ironic conflict between the overt ground rules of propriety and the more covert ground rules of lust provides the emotional energy discharged in laughter.

The dis-expected, of course, occurs frequently in the fantastic. The diametric reconfigurations of the fantastic provide ample opportunity for jokes. However, these jokes need not in themselves be fantastic occurrences:

> "Well!" thought Alice to herself, "after such a fall as this [down the rabbit-hole], I shall think nothing of tumbling down the stairs! How brave they'll all think me at home! Why, I wouldn't say anything about it, even if I fell off the top of the house!" (which was very likely true.)[9]

---

[7] Arthur Koestler, *Insight and Outlook*, University of Nebraska Press, Lincoln, 1949, chapters 2 and 3, one of the most incisive psychological analyses of the bases of laughter.

[8] *Ibid.*, p. 32.

[9] Lewis Carroll, *Alice's Adventures in Wonderland*, p. 27.

On the other hand, if Alice were to say something "about it" *after* breaking her neck, that would be fantastic. We enter a narrative world with the preconceptions of our arm-chair world intact, and these preconceptions only change as the narrative reconfigures them. In our world, and in Wonderland, the dead do not speak. Their speaking is un-expected in the sense of *anti-expected*. When the anti-ex-pected happens, we are in the presence of the fantastic.

The occurrence of the anti-expected can be fantastic even if it takes place in a work that is not itself a fantasy. In *Candide*, Voltaire has Cunegonde say clearly in chapter 8 that she witnessed the Bulgarians as "they murdered my father and brother and cut my mother to pieces."[10] But in chapter 14, we have a recognition scene full of quite as much re-ported astonishment as ever Alice felt:

> "Heavens! Is it possible!" cried the Commandant.
> "What a miracle!" cried Candide.
> "Can it be you?" said the Commandant.
> " 'Tis impossible!" said Candide. They both fell over backwards, embraced and shed rivers of tears.
> "What! Can it be you, reverend father? You, the fair Cunegonde's brother! You, who were killed by the Bul-garians! You . . . The World is indeed a strange place."[11]

This excessive show of surprise in part beats home sublim-inally the point that fantastic good fortune, which this res-urrection represents, does not ordinarily occur in life. At the moment of reading the recognition dialogue, we experi-ence satire by exaggeration, even though in the next mo-ment the brother naturalizes the fantastic by the simple as-

---

[10] Jean François Marie Arouet de Voltaire, *Candide*, Richard Al-dington, transl., Hanover House, Garden City, New York, 1959, p. 26.
[11] *Ibid.*, p. 45.

sertion that his wound, though indeed terrible, simply was not fatal. This satire is part of Voltaire's central attack on Leibniz's notion that ours is the best of all possible worlds. Here that point is made by a brief use of the fantastic.

Nathanael West provides us with a similar occurrence in *A Cool Million*. This satire on American values is an episodic inversion of the Horatio Alger story of luck, pluck, and decency. Lemuel Pitkin is decent enough—like Pinocchio, all his sins can be attributed to bad counselors rather than bad intentions—and plucky enough—as we will see—but his luck is all bad. In the first episode he loses his money, in the second his teeth, in the third his thumb, and so on ever upward—or is it downward? At one point, he is even attacked by Indians!

> With [Chief] Satinpenny leading them, the warriors galloped through the forest . . . [and] found Lem still fast in the unrelenting jaws of the bear trap.
>
> "Yeehoieee!" screamed the chief, as he stooped over the recumbent form of the poor lad and tore the scalp from his head. Then brandishing his reeking trophy on high, he sprang on his pony and made for the nearest settlements, followed on his pony by his horde of blood-crazed savages. . . .
>
> With a curse unbecoming one of his few years, [an Indian boy] left off [fire-making] to go swimming in the creek, first looting Lem's bloody head of its store teeth and glass eye.[12]

Our preconceptions from the armchair world tell us that Lem is dead; we might say that his continued existence is anti-expected. However, Lem has lived through so much al-

[12] Nathanael West, *A Cool Million*, Avon Books, New York, 1969 (1931), p. 87.

ready that we can accept it when we are told that a Mr. Whipple "bent over the unconscious form."[13] Lemuel Pitkin's tenacity is implied at the covert level of the narrative, and the anti-expected is seen to be merely the dis-expected. Lem's survival is fantastic, but this particular report of his survival is merely an additional element in a satire that proceeds by ever escalating the occurrence of the dis-expected. Because so many of our perspectives enter a narrative with us (for instance, that scalping is fatal), fiction often conflates the anti-expected and the dis-expected. West does not, of course, actually say that Lem has been killed by the Indians.

The relationships among the several senses of *unexpected* can perhaps best be expressed by a geometric metaphor. The truly fantastic occurs when the ground rules of a narrative are forced to make a 180° reversal, when prevailing perspectives are directly contradicted. This is true, even if the effect lasts only a moment (as in *Candide*), and is true whether the reversal occurs in a Fantasy or not. Less complete reversals, say a 90° turnabout (like the dis-expected punch line of a joke) or a 120° turnabout (like the highly dis-expected survival of Lemuel Pitkin), participate in the complex of feelings of surprise, shock, delight, fear, and so on that marks the fantastic, but are not themselves truly fantastic; they are flavored by the fantastic. The dis-expected then is in part not-expected, in part anti-expected. Jokes always give us the dis-expected, and most other narratives too depend somewhat on fulfilling expectations we didn't know we had. When Woodcourt marries Esther at the end of *Bleak House*, though we had been distracted from this possibility by the plenitude of other involvements, it somehow rings true, it keeps with Dickens' comic decorum. As the dis-expected becomes a more and more complete

[13] *Ibid.*, p. 88.

reversal of the ground rules of the narrative world, however, the dis-expected approaches the diametric reversal of the anti-expected, a hallmark of the fantastic. As long as a text first makes us accept the notion that flowers cannot talk, their talking will strike us as fantastic.

Besides the anti-expected, the dis-expected, and the not-expected, we still have one other kind of occurrence that is non-normal in a narrative: the irrelevant. Irrelevant occurrences violate a basic ground rule of all art: every element of a work of art tends toward the organic impact of that work of art. If this rule were reversible, we might well have a new source of the fantastic. However, it is not. Let us distinguish between the apparently irrelevant and the truly irrelevant. The apparently irrelevant that functions co-operatively within the narrative (for instance, the telling, witty *non sequitur*) actually obeys the rule of organic wholeness, and is thus not irrelevant at all. Long arguments have been marshalled to show, for instance, that the interpolated stories in *Tom Jones* and *Don Quixote* are only apparently irrelevant, and indeed actually tend through this appearance of irrelevance to further develop the main narratives, both of which depend in part on a confusion of appearance and reality (Tom, who appears a pauper, is an heir; Quixote, who sees himself as a knight, is actually a broken-down country gentleman). In their confusion of the relevant and the irrelevant, such interpolated stories support—and at a higher level are relevant to—the main themes of the works in which they occur. In this sense, apparently irrelevant occurrences have no necessary connection with the fantastic.

On the other hand, there is no reason why apparently irrelevant occurrences might not be fantastic. In *The Cherry Orchard* the mystic twanging sound heard off-stage three times during the play and never explained is a fantastic occurrence. The entire play, dependent as it is on commercial values, middle-class morality, and so on, continually reaffirms a set of ground rules that make supernal portents anti-expected. The apparently irrelevant, then, is not in art actually irrelevant; the apparently irrelevant may or may not be involved in the fantastic.

One should further note that the truly irrelevant tends to be excluded not only from art but in some sense from all experience. Edmund Carpenter reports this of the Canadian Eskimos:

> I once naively thought my Eskimo hosts would be fascinated to hear about the remarkable world from which I came. In fact, they showed only irritation when I talked about it. If a tubercular Eskimo is taken from his igloo and put in a sanatorium in Brandon, Manitoba, or Hamilton, Ontario, and treated there for four years, gradually being given freedom to wander about the hospital and town, when he returns home, it's unlikely he will ever mention a single thing he witnessed or learned. The outside world is uncertain, dangerous, hostile—above all, alien, untranslatable.[14]

The key term here is "untranslatable." Where there is no frame of reference, no set of perspectives waiting to be fulfilled, assaulted, or reversed, man apprehends almost nothing. As McLuhan says, "I wouldn't have seen it if I hadn't believed it." Every society selects its own aberrations: for certain Canadian Indian tribes, the savage windigo psychosis; for northern Europeans, schizophrenia. Conversely, Winnebagos do not split their personalities, and Irishmen, despite Jonathan Swift, do not cannibalize their families.

The fantastic is a direct reversal of ground rules, and

[14] Edmund Carpenter, *Oh, What a Blow That Phantom Gave Me!* Holt, Rinehart and Winston, New York, 1972, pp. 53-54.

therefore is in part determined by those ground rules. The truly irrelevant has nothing to do with ground rules, and therefore can no more be fantastic than it can be realistic. One may define the fantastic in part as "conceived or appearing as if conceived by an unrestrained imagination"[15] only so long as we remember that all imaginations are restrained at least by the perspectives necessary to create a work of narrative art. As Gestalt psychology teaches us, there is no narrative world, any more than there is a physical world, without a set of ground rules by which to perceive it.

One immediately sees that the dependence of the fantastic on ground rules leaves open the distressing possibility that we might not, in reading a given text, recognize those reversals for what they are. The case of Daniel Defoe illustrates this. Defoe himself was an ardent Dissenter, son of a Dissenter and schooled at the Dissenting academy at Newington Green.[16] Of his over four hundred attributed works, only one, *The Shortest Way with the Dissenters* (1702), seems clearly intended to be ironic. This work is what Gilbert Highet calls an "ironic monologue,"[17] in which the speaking voice mimes—and usually distorts by exaggeration—the voice of the ironist's enemy. In this case, Defoe came out so powerfully against the Dissenters that many churchmen mistook his meaning as serious. As Vonnegut says, "we are what we pretend to be, so we must be careful about what we pretend to be."[18] Defoe was not sufficiently careful, and the writer of *The Shortest Way with the Dis-*

---

[15] *The Random House Dictionary of the English Language*, unabridged edition, New York, 1966.

[16] Alan Dugald McKillop, *English Literature from Dryden to Burns*, Appleton-Century-Crofts, New York, 1948, pp. 146ff.

[17] Gilbert Highet, *The Anatomy of Satire*, Princeton University Press, Princeton, New Jersey, 1962, pp. 55ff.

[18] Kurt Vonnegut, Jr., *Mother Night*, Avon, New York, 1961, p. v.

*senters* was widely assumed to be a Tory churchman. When the truth became known, public fury was so great that Defoe was imprisoned and released a year later, only after he concluded what seems to have been a somewhat shady deal with Tory leader Harley. As Ian Watt observes, Defoe's "only conscious exercise in irony, in fact, was indeed a masterpiece . . . not of irony but of impersonation."[19] In 1702, Daniel Defoe did not make ground rules clear.

Similarly, we must consider modern readings of Defoe's lusty *Moll Flanders*. Many readers enjoy the subtle irony of the whore protesting against the whoring life, of the criminal—writing from her Virginia estate—asserting that crime does not pay. However, many other readers steeped in Defoe's life, works, and times find it incredible that the author could have intended this irony. This problem

> would seem to be a matter not of literary criticism but of social history. We cannot today believe that so intelligent a man as Defoe should have viewed either his heroine's economic attitudes or her pious protestations with anything other than derision. Defoe's other writings, however, do not support this belief, and it may be surmised that the course of history has brought about in us powerful and often unconscious predispositions to regard certain matters ironically which Defoe and his age treated quite seriously.[20]

How, indeed, is one to know? Defoe's contemporaries mistook him at least once, and some of us apparently mistake him today, yet his writing holds together marvelously: Moll and Robinson Crusoe still delight readers everywhere. So much depends upon perspective. In East Africa today, the

[19] Ian Watt, *The Rise of the Novel*, University of California Press, Berkeley, 1965 (1957), p. 126.
[20] *Ibid.*, p. 127.

rhinoceros is in danger of extinction by poachers.[21] They seek only the horn which, ground into powder, will fetch several thousand dollars in the Orient, where it is believed to be an aphrodisiac. Of course, the Orientals would never believe that rhinoceros horn, which is really only a mass of dermal filaments, has sexual potency. No indeed. They believe that sexual potency resides in the horn of the unicorn. Perhaps Borges' *Celestial Emporium* is not so fantastic as it seems.

Fortunately, we can rest assured that the *Celestial Emporium* is at least in part fantastic. The category of "stray dogs" is surely whimsical, but even granting dissent here too, the inserted category of "others," like the category of "those that are included in this classification," allows for fantastic anti-expectations in a purely intra-textual way. One way for a writer to signal us across time and space that he intends the fantastic is to give us examples of it (such as "others") that depend on diametrical reversal of purely structural ground rules. To this type of clue, in essence a message from the implied author, we can add two other surprisingly widespread, though not quite as sure, signals of the fantastic: a character's astonishment and the statements of the narrator. By these three types of signal, despite the case of Defoe and the very real problems of knowing narrative ground rules, we can identify the fantastic.

We have already seen the fantastic signalled by the surprise of a character caught in a fantastic occurrence both when we saw Alice's astonishment and when we saw Candide's effusive recognition of his beloved's brother. This recognition scene, however, might have been created by an author intending to satirize not Leibniz but, say, the my-isn't-it-a-small-world syndrome. How many times have we

[21] Louis S. B. Leakey, *Animals of East Africa*, National Geographic Society, Washington, D.C., 1969, p. 38.

heard, and even said, "Imagine running into you here!" "The world is indeed a strange place." One might easily become annoyed at hearing the same stock phrases again and again when the situation these phrases are intended to meet is by definition highly unusual: our pitiful reliance on cliché, the satirist may imply, is yet another example of the paucity of human invention. To know, then, that Voltaire's scene is fantastic as well as satiric, one must recall that a presumably reliable source had reported the brother's death, and one must further bring into the narrative world the view of the armchair world that the dead do not speak.

In the same way, one must have a certain perspective to interpret as fantastic the following case of astonishment from William Morris' great utopian vision, *News From Nowhere* (1890):

> I found myself saying, almost against my will, "How old is [the bridge]?"
>
> "O, not very old," he said; "it was built, or at least opened, in 2003. There used to be a rather plain timber bridge before then."
>
> The date shut my mouth as if a key had been turned in a padlock fixed to my lips; for I saw that something inexplicable had happened.[22]

That inexplicable thing, never explained in Morris' communist tract, is time travel, a notion that the perspectives of our armchair world make entirely fantastic. However, the passage need not be so read. Time travel is apparently acceptable as a learnable skill by some Scientologists.[23]

In many works, for instance Hawthorne's *Blithedale Ro-*

---

[22] William Morris, *News From Nowhere*, James Redmond, ed., Routledge & Kegan Paul, London, 1970, p. 6.

[23] L. Ron Hubbard, *Dianetics*, Paperback Library, New York, 1950, pp. 220-230.

*mance*, we have perfectly normal occurrences that appear to the narrator as fantastic merely because these occurrences are inexplicable *to him*. However, the implied author provides clues by which the reader can be one up on such narrators as Miles Coverdale and can know whether the required explanation is natural or supernatural. In the Morris case the clue seems overt: we are given one date (2003) that clearly could not occur in past tense for someone writing in 1890, a time when, as we know historically—that is, extra-textually—time travel was not thought to be possible. But how do we know that this book really is from that period? We have, of course, the publication date inside the book; but more importantly, we have the language of the book itself. Only by our training in the usages of language are we correctly able to interpret astonishment signals as marking the fantastic.

In *Writing Degree Zero* (1953), Roland Barthes propounds the notion of *écriture*, or *writing degree*. This is a centrally important notion for solving problems of referentiality in written language, and hence for dealing with questions of real-world truth in considering the fantastic. Barthes reminds us of Saussure's distinction between *langue* (language) and *parole* (speech). The *langue* exists in the abstract and consists of a set of grammatical rules sufficient to generate an infinite number of sentences plus a lexicon designed to be used by that language's grammar. As a language, then, English is reducible to a set of principles and a dictionary, and all the utterances and writings that have ever occurred in English or ever will occur are merely examples of English at work. Each of these examples is a *parole*.

*Langue* and *parole* are fundamentally different kinds of phenomena, Saussure argues. All native speakers of a language are "competent" in that language; yet any speaker of a language is entirely likely to misspeak himself, to make a "performance" error. Fortunately, all speakers of a language are subliminally aware of the distinction between performance and competence. When we hear someone make a performance error (*parole*) in English (*langue*), we who are ourselves competent in English can correct that performance error in our minds (exactly as we can see past a stupid narrator). "What did you said?" "I said, your assumption that I'm speaking English and your own competence in the *langue* allows you to correct and thereby understand my *parole*." Even if the question is put ungrammatically.

Dialects are subsets of a language. They too have a grammar, usually a somewhat more restricting set of rules than that of the overall *langue*, and they frequently have a special lexicon, or special lexical rules, or at least indigenous idioms, that mark *paroles* as coming uniquely from that dialect. "How's by you?" exhibits all these traits for the dialect of a class of Americans who are themselves emigrants from Eastern Europe or the children of those emigrants. Such an utterance is a perfectly correct *parole* within the dialect spoken by that group. The recognition of that dialect by a hearer, regardless of what is actually said, vivifies the set of perspectives that the hearer has learned to associate with speakers of that dialect. What Barthes noticed is that there is a written equivalent for dialect that also carries with it a set of perspectives. He calls these subsets of language *écritures* (writing degrees), but to follow the usage of most English-speaking linguists and the model of *dialect*, it is perhaps easiest to call these written subsets of language *grapholects*. Like dialects, grapholects mark the writing "voice" as coming from a particular time, place, and social group. The date of publication may or may not be active in one's mind during the reading of any given text, but the grapholect of that text, and the associated set of perspectives it vivifies, is always present.

Returning to Morris, we readers automatically place his grapholect, though justifying this placement is a long and difficult task.[24] If we could examine the process by which our minds locate a grapholect, it might be seen like this: "The date shut my mouth as if a key had been turned in a padlock fixed to my lips; for I saw that something inexplicable had happened." The imagery and querulousness seem too modern for early nineteenth century—Austen or Scott, say—yet too old for the frankness and pregnancy of even such early twentieth-century authors as Joyce or Lawrence; in fact, the grapholect that uses "something inexplicable" and employs mechanical images with this (writing) degree of delicacy is more a compromise between the grapholect of H. G. Wells (*The Time Machine*, 1895) and that of George Eliot (*Middlemarch*, 1872). We read the signal of the character's astonishment as indicating the fantastic, therefore, not merely because he is astonished, but because our unconsciously vivified perspectives on the world of his grapholect imply that his astonishment, unlike Coverdale's, comes not from obtuseness but from the shock of experiencing the anti-expected: in 1890, the year whose perspectives the reading keeps before us, time travel was fantastic.

In his densely ironic narrative called *The Warlord of the Air: A Scientific Romance*, Michael Moorcock makes extraordinary use of the power of the grapholect to keep preconceptions alive. The Edgar Rice Burroughs title and the H. G. Wells subtitle rightly predict that this novel will be written in a turn-of-the-century grapholect. However, the

---

[24] One excellent effort to describe a dialect in detail is Walter A. Wolfram, *A Sociolinguistic Description of Detroit Negro Speech*, Center for Applied Linguistics, Washington, D. C., 1969. This work is well over two hundred pages in length.

book was actually published in 1971. According to Moorcock's editorial comments, he is presenting a narrative taken from a manuscript he has just discovered in the personal effects of his grandfather Moorcock, a manuscript dictated to that grandfather in 1902 by a strange, lost, Lord Jim character named Bastable, who claims he had been transported into 1973 and has returned.[25] Moorcock's 1973, of course, is surprisingly similar to our own—and yet different. By these similarities (for instance, there is an irascible scout leader named Ronnie Reagan), Moorcock's editorial comments are seen for the window dressing they are. His narrative structure parallels More's in *Utopia*, with the added twists that utopia is now in the future, but a future already known to be impossible—indeed, for post-1973 readers, a future known to be past. This inherently fantastic temporal perspective infects the narrative throughout, and would serve to keep the narrative world at least fantastic; however, the fantastic is used here in conjunction with the perspectives imposed by the grapholect to make the work satiric as well.

Bastable is knocked unconscious and awakens to his first sight of woman circa 1973, the far future!

I would not be a man, with a man's instincts, if I did not admit I had been both surprised and delighted at the appearance of my nurse. It had only been a glimpse, but it showed me just how much things had changed since 1902. The nurse's uniform had been starched white and blue, with a stiff cap on her neatly pinned auburn hair. A fairly ordinary nurse's uniform save for one thing: her skirt was at least *twelve inches* clear of

[25] It is hardly coincidental that Wells' hero of *Men Like Gods* (1923), who drives his auto off into the fourth dimension and ultimately back again, is named Barnstaple. Both characters likely derive from Edith Nesbit's once popular stories of the Bastable children, including Oswald.

the floor and revealed the prettiest pair of calves, the neatest set of ankles I had ever seen off the stage of The Empire, Leicester Square! It certainly gave the nurse greater freedom of movement and was, essentially, practical. I wondered if all women were dressed in this practical and attractive way. If so, I could see unexpected pleasures arising from my unwitting trip into the Future![26]

Bastable's poor attempt to hide his prurience, and our own recognition that today a woman is as likely to have her skirt twelve inches "clear of" the knee, combine to gently satirize the Victorian mores called to mind and to humble us, through our own sympathetic response to this prurience, by a reminder that in the real 1973 we did find short skirts rather "attractive." And very practical? A contemporary character arguing for the utility of the miniskirt might well seem silly, but a wanderer from the past, ah, that is another story—and a fantastic one. Bastable's authority as a man from the past is continually validated by the grapholect of the novel.[27]

We see then that interpreting a character's astonishment is based on our total understanding of the narrative world, an understanding that not only grows from attention to the

[26] Michael Moorcock, *The Warlord of the Air*, Ace Books, New York, 1971, p. 55.

[27] This delightful book is full of unusual reversals made possible by its fantastic temporal structure. There are characters, for instance, named Korzienowski and Ulianov, the former an airship captain, the latter a failed revolutionary. From our vantage beyond the real 1973, we know that the real Korzienowski changed his name to Conrad and became an author, while the real Ulianov changed his name to Lenin and became a premier. Both these historical figures abandoned their real names for fictional ones. In Moorcock's fantastic "future," he makes up parallel fictional characters who use not the fictional names but the real ones. This twist in Moorcock's text is, I believe, the sole literary example of this particular type of diametric reversal.

overt action reported in the text, but that intimately involves the perspectives unconsciously vivified by the grapholect in which the narrative is presented. By the same token, we accept a narrator's assertion of the fantastic only when this does not contradict the possibilities for the fantastic carried by the grapholect. Norton Juster's children's fantasy, *The Phantom Tollbooth*, is written in a grapholect we might call mid-twentieth-century dull: "There was once a boy named Milo who didn't know what to do with himself. . . ."[28] When Juster's narrator asserts that "What had started as make-believe was now very real,"[29] the diametric reversal of the mundane perspectives of the grapholect signals the fantastic. On the other hand, when a narrator in a men's magazine story describes a woman as having "a fantastic body," he may mean that her body is unusually well endowed, but not well endowed with tentacles. This astonishment does not signal the truly fantastic, and we know as much from both the grapholect of the magazine and the decorum of the story.

We have then three classes of signal for the fantastic: signals of the characters (such as Alice's astonishment), signals of the narrator (such as Juster's and Morris' assertions), and signals of the implied author (such as the narrative structures of Borges and Moorcock). Each of these three types of signal may occur in any given work (for example, in *News From Nowhere* the astonished character is also the narrator, and the future history structure is itself fantastic); however, each class of signal can be properly interpreted only by reference to the ground rules of the narrative world, ground rules that are foisted upon the reader in large part by his whole life's training in the reading of lit-

---

[28] Norton Juster, *The Phantom Tollbooth*, Random House, New York, 1967 (1961), p. 9.
[29] *Ibid.*, p. 16.

erature and its many grapholects. Without the clarity in these signals afforded by definitive reference to a grapholect, the fantastic is often mistaken for something else; Defoe goes to jail.

In addition to the reader's habitual responses to grapholects, ground rules are also shaped by playing on the reader's whole experience. The notion that the dead do not speak is such a ground rule, but early on in *A Very Private Life*, Michael Frayn's highly entertaining future-tense narration of a fairy tale heroine in a horrid utopia, we learn that death is not permanent.

> "Do you die when you get old, Mummy?" Uncumber will ask one day.
> "Sometimes," her mother replies.
> "What happens to you when you die?"
> "Oh, you take some special medicine, and you get better again."
> "But *I* mean, if you really, *really* die?"
> "Well, if you really die very badly...."[30]

The mother continues the explanation, but we need not. What we see here is that in treating death in this fantastic way, Frayn has in part created a new grapholect, a new sub-set of English, appropriate to his novel, in which the word *death* no longer vivifies the set of perspectives which it does in standard English of the 1970s. In so doing, for the duration of the reading, Frayn teaches us a new way to look at death. This function of the fantastic is educational in the root sense: it leads one from darkness to light, it creates in the mind a diametric reversal and opens up new and fantastic worlds.

In the third chapter of *Through the Looking Glass*, Alice

[30] Michael Frayn, *A Very Private Life*, Viking, New York, 1968, p. 7.

finds herself in a wood in which she can't even remember her own name. She meets a talking Fawn who also cannot identify itself.

> So they walked on together through the wood, Alice with her arms clasped lovingly round the soft neck of the Fawn, till they came out into another open field, and here the Fawn gave a sudden bound into the air, and shook itself free from Alice's arm. "I'm a Fawn!" it cried out in a voice of delight. "And, dear me! you're a human child!" A sudden look of alarm came into its beautiful brown eyes, and in another moment it had darted away at full speed.[31]

This passage teaches us something important about the way names carry perspectives with them. Names are just one class of words. The fantastic takes words and reconfigures their semantic ranges, puts them in new contexts, creates new grapholects for them, and in so doing it liberates us.

Hawthorne explained why one might indulge in the fantastic in his preface to *The House of the Seven Gables*, a work which depends on, among other elements, the actual operation of a family curse. In 1851, "Romance" referred to such works as Horace Walpole's *The Castle of Otranto*, in which we find hauntings, eerie sounds, and murder by supernaturally dropping a forty-foot-high battle helmet on a groom-to-be, all items we might well call fantastic.[32] Hawthorne wrote:

[31] Lewis Carroll, *Through the Looking Glass*, p. 227.
[32] Clara Reeve, *The Progress of Romance* (1785), is the first important attempt to distinguish between novel and romance. The two types of narrative, Reeve argues, require two separate standards of evaluation. Her survey of English prose is intended as a validation of *The Castle of Otranto* and such other works as *The Champion of Virtue, a Gothic Story* (1777), by Clara Reeve.

When a writer calls his work a Romance, it need hardly be observed that he wishes to claim a certain latitude, both as to its fashion and material, which he would not have felt himself entitled to assume had he professed to be writing a Novel. The latter form of composition is presumed to aim at a very minute fidelity, not merely to the possible, but to the probable and ordinary course of man's experience. The former—while, as a work of art, it must rigidly subject itself to laws, and while it sins unpardonably so far as it may swerve aside from the truth of the human heart—has fairly a right to present that truth under circumstances, to a great extent, of the writer's own choosing or creation. If he think fit, also, he may so manage his atmospherical medium as to bring out or mellow the light and deepen and enrich the shadows of the picture. He will be wise, no doubt, to make a very moderate use of the privileges here stated, and, especially, to mingle the Marvellous rather as a slight, delicate, and evanescent flavor, than as any portion of the actual substance of the dish offered to the public. He can hardly be said, however, to commit a literary crime even if he disregard this caution.[33]

The fantastic is to be used to reveal "the truth of the human heart."

One of the most accepted of the truths of the human heart is that we often conceive ourselves, and act, as if we had two natures: a base, evil, nighttime nature and a fine, good, daytime nature. Some trace this dichotomy to Calvin-

[33] Nathaniel Hawthorne, Preface to *The House of the Seven Gables*, in *The Complete Novels and Selected Tales of Nathaniel Hawthorne*, Norman Holmes Pearson, ed., Modern Library, New York, 1937, p. 243.

ism, others to "basic human nature." The evidence of cultural anthropology probably will not bear out this latter contention, but surely enough of us have been created in the wake of Calvin to assert that the conflict between man's nighttime and daytime selves is *a* truth of *many* human hearts. This truth might, of course, be treated in many ways, but the treatments we remember are those which, like the truth itself, depend on day and night, 180° oppositions. Indeed, if we wish to label a person in whom we see this conflict between two natures as particularly strong, we call him a Jekyll-and-Hyde. Similarly, perhaps no literary image of alienation is more potent than that of Gregor Samsa, Kafka's man-turned-dung-beetle. Although the dictionary may define the fantastic as "not real or based on reality,"[34] the fantastic is important precisely because it is wholly dependent on reality for its existence. Admittedly, the fantastic is reality turned precisely 180° around, but this is reality nonetheless, a fantastic narrative reality that speaks the truth of the human heart.

Understanding then what the fantastic is, how we recognize it, and what are some of its powers, we can begin to explore its relation to narrative generally. As we have already seen, many works which we would not call Fantasies (satires, for example) make important use of the fantastic; however, the fantastic is clearly the central quality in works we would unequivocally call Fantasies (for example, *Through the Looking Glass*). I would like to suggest that we can profitably consider narratives as arrayed along a continuum, ordered in terms of increasing use of the fantastic, with true Fantasies as the polar extreme. (In capitalizing *Fantasy*, I wish to identify a particular genre whose defining characteristics will shortly become clear; in referring to the *fantastic*, I intend to recall those structural properties we have discussed of the diametric reversal of the

---

[34] *Random House Dictionary of the English Language.*

ground rules of a narrative world and the peculiar range of emotional affects associated with such reversals; by using *fantasy*, uncapitalized, I mean the lay definition, which includes the psychologist's ideas about wish fulfillment and so on.) This hypothesis can be stated in an alternate fashion: the fantastic has a place in any narrative genre, but that genre to which the fantastic is exhaustively central is the class of narratives we call Fantasy. Some examples, I hope, will make this notion clear.

Chinua Achebe's *Things Fall Apart* is a classic of modern Africa, a moving story of one over-proud man trying to resist culture shock, and failing. The stable and supportive world of the Ibos is threatened by the increasing proximity of the white man. In the following passage, the white man is not yet perceived as a threat. The men of the tribe are discussing the nature of the world, a world large enough to contain even the fantastic. Note the diametric up-down and black-white reversals:

"The world is large," said Okonkwo. "I have even heard that in some tribes a man's children belong to his wife and her family."

"That cannot be," said Machi. "You might as well say that the woman lies on top of the man when they are making the children."

"It is like the story of white men who, they say, are white like this piece of chalk," said Obierika. . . . "And these white men, they say, have no toes."

"And have you never seen them?" asked Machi.

"Have you?" asked Obierika.

"One of them passes here frequently," said Machi. "His name is Amadi."

Those who knew Amadi laughed. He was a leper, and the polite name for leprosy was "the white skin."[35]

[35] Chinua Achebe, *Things Fall Apart*, Fawcett, Greenwich, Conn., 1959, p. 71.

There is a very gentle use of the fantastic here. The unbelief of Obierika tells us readers that the white man is an anti-expected phenomenon in the world of these characters. The disjunction between covert and overt ground rules that produces the conflict released in the laughter at Machi's joke is the disjunction between taking a phenomenon as anti-expected and taking it as dis-expected. In this key passage, what is at first fantastic to the Ibos makes its first step toward becoming all too possible. Although at this early point in the novel the association of white men with disease is satiric, by the end of the novel, after the demoralizing of these individual Ibos and the total eradication of their tribal social structure, the disease image can be seen as prophetic. Achebe's book is not very fantastic, but it does use the fantastic to make its point.

George S. Schuyler's *Black No More* (1931) uses a similar joke, but here the joke informs the entire world of the novel. Dr. Junius Crookman, a black physician aiming for "chromatic democracy"[36] and "chromatic emancipation,"[37] has discovered a method of turning black people into white people. This method does not merely change skin color, but also changes the facial features slightly so that a black person becomes truly white, not merely whitened. This fantastic phenomenon is ostensibly naturalized in a press conference Crookman holds:

". . . during my first year at college I noticed a black girl on the street one day who had several irregular white patches on her face and hands . . . a nervous disease known as vitiligo. . . . It absolutely removes skin pigment and sometimes it turns a Negro completely white but only after a period of thirty or forty years. It

[36] George S. Schuyler, *Black No More*, Collier, New York, 1971 (1931), p. 64.
[37] *Ibid.*, p. 87.

occurred to me that if one could discover some means of artificially inducing and stimulating this nervous disease at will, one might possibly solve the American race problem."[38]

Schuyler, a black man himself, is perhaps having Machi's fun here: vitiligo is not a nervous disease, but a variety of leprosy.

The joke, detected or not, underlies the whole book, a satire directed as much against blacks as it is against whites. Crookman the crusader continues his press conference:

"My sociology teacher had once said that there were but three ways for the Negro to solve his problem in America, . . . 'To either get out, get white or get along.' Since he wouldn't and couldn't get out and was getting along only differently [sic], it seemed to me that the only thing for him was to get white."[39]

Crookman becomes a predictive satire on Hitler, and a brother of Swift's modest projector, when he says that "if there were no Negroes, there could be no Negro problem."[40] This whole method of problem solving (one can prevent death from abdominal bleeding by applying a tourniquet at the neck) has the structure of the fantastic: there is no *solution* to the "Negro problem" if there is no problem (and death is not prevented if it is precipitated). Since this black-white reversal sets the atmosphere and motivates many of the plot elements of the book, one would say that *Black No More* is more fantastic than *Things Fall Apart*.

However, *Black No More* is not a Fantasy. Its main plot follows all the conventions and plays with all the expectations that underlie formula fiction of the *True Romances* variety, merely employing those conventions with an at-

[38] *Ibid.*, pp. 26-27.   [39] *Ibid.*   [40] *Ibid.*, p. 54.

mospheric twist. Max Discher, our hero, is an incorrigible, likeable man-about-Harlem who likes his women the lighter the better. Sitting alone in a nightclub he spots HER, "a tall, slim, titian-haired girl who had seemingly stepped from heaven or the front cover of a magazine."[41] Max, of course, is smitten with her. He askes her to dance, but she cruelly rejects him. Max, however, will not give up. He is the very first American black to take Dr. Crookman's treatment. He has overheard the girl mention folks in Atlanta and as soon as Max Discher, now Matthew Fischer, is white, he heads south. There he plays upon his abilities as a fast-talking con man and attempts to land a "job" as a double-agent rabble-rouser and major organizer behind Rev. Henry Givens' Knights of Nordica, a hate society sucking in money from gullible bigots who are afraid that "white niggers" are going to create a rash of very anti-expected black babies. Matthew cynically wants to act the saviour of the white race. His major test is securing Givens' confidence, and to do this he must hold a successful rally. Givens tells his wife to come to the portentous event, and even tells her to bring their daughter Helen. Now who, gentle reader, might Helen be? Could it be so? Will it? We must wait seven full pages, we must see Matthew notice the girl in the audience, he must suddenly, while speaking, realize he has seen her before, he must finish his speech, he must ask Givens to identify the young woman, and only then, irony of ironies, will we hear the long awaited words: "Why that there's my daughter, Helen. Like to meet her?"[42]

The romantic structure of *Black No More* decisively marks its genre. It may be reasonably objected that a structure built on such coincidences is itself fantastic, and this is certainly so. However, such coincidence is, after all, an

[41] *Ibid.*, p. 20.  [42] *Ibid.*, p. 79.

integral part of *all* narrative, no matter how well that coincidence seems naturalized by the exposition of motivation. The universe around us is chaos; art is ordered. To that extent, all art is fantastic. But *Black No More*, though more fantastic than *Things Fall Apart*, is still not itself a Fantasy.

One might look for a Fantasy among fairy tales. They are, clearly, more fantastic than even such fantastic satires as *Black No More*. Where Schuyler's narrative world, with its one central exception, shares the perspectives of our armchair world, a fairy tale has a whole set of perspectives that exist in another world altogether. Tolkien names this land Faerie, and defines fairy tales this way:

> ... a "fairy-story" is one which touches on or uses Faerie, whatever its own main purpose may be: satire, adventure, morality, fantasy.[43]

By this phrasing, Tolkien first makes a point he will make over and over: fairy tales are not true Fantasies, though they may contain what he calls fantasy, an aspect of imaginative subcreation present in all art. He continues:

> Faerie itself may perhaps most nearly be translated by Magic—but it is magic of a peculiar mood and power, and at the furthest pole from the vulgar devices of the laborious, scientific, magician.[44]

Later in the essay, Tolkien renames this Magic and calls it Enchantment.[45] Faerie then becomes the World of Enchantment. When we enter Schuyler's narrative world, we make one fantastic reversal: we assume blacks can become white; when we enter the world of a fairy tale, we trade in a host of real world perspectives.

[43] Tolkien, *The Tolkien Reader*, p. 10.
[44] *Ibid.*          [45] *Ibid.*, p. 52.

"Briar Rose" ("Sleeping Beauty") is a fine example of a fairy tale. Notice how it begins:

A long time ago, there lived a King and Queen, who said every day, "If only we had a child"; but for a long time they had none.

It fell out once, as the Queen was bathing, that a frog crept out of the water on to the land, and said to her: "Your wish shall be fulfilled: before a year has passed you shall bring a daughter into the world."

The frog's words came true.[46]

Here is the World of Enchantment. This is a world clearly more fantastic than Schuyler's, or more fantastic than that of any document that pretends to social realism. However, here we find the "truth of the human heart" nonetheless. Cirlot points out that, because water is a universal symbol of female fecundity, the frog, which bridges the elements of water and land, is itself a symbol of fecundity.[47] In the sense of archetypal psychological fantasy, the frog's prophecy rings true in large part because it is uttered by a frog. In literary terms, the frog's prophecy rings true because it is uttered in the World of Enchantment, a world we know we have entered because we've already passed the welcome signs: "A long time ago there lived a King and Queen." As Max Lüthi writes in his chapter on "Sleeping Beauty":

. . . the fairy tale does not portray the abnormal case, but natural development, and it fills its hearers with confidence that a new, larger life is to come after the

[46] ———, "Briar Rose," from "Seven Fairy Tales by The Brothers Grimm," in Once Upon A Time: The Fairy Tale World of Arthur Rackham, Margery Darrell, ed., Viking, New York, 1972, p. 51.
[47] J. E. Cirlot, A Dictionary of Symbols, Jack Sage, transl., Philosophical Library, New York, 1962, p. 109.

deathlike sleep—that, after the isolation [felt during sexual maturation], a new form of contact and community will follow.[48]

It rings absolutely true that the whole castle is rejuvenated by the first kiss of Briar Rose and her fated lover. They carry on life, and perpetuate both our world and the World of Enchantment.

In the first incident of this tale, the Queen, unlike Alice in the garden of talking flowers, shows no astonishment at the talking frog. We do not find here the signals of the fantastic. This is not Wonderland but the less energetic and less frantic World of Enchantment. In this world, fairies are invited to christenings, there are foreknown rules for how much one fairy's spell can offset another's, and the prophecy of the pricked finger is as believed, and as confirmed, as the frog's prophecy of Briar Rose's birth. Within the World of Enchantment, everything happens according to rule. To William Morris, writing captions for Edward Burne-Jones' illustrations for "Briar Rose," this stability of rule went by the name of fate:

> The fateful slumber floats and flows
> About the tangle of the rose;
> But lo! the fated hand and heart
> To rend the slumbrous curse apart![49]

Lüthi too remarks that fairy tales, and their heroes, live in a world with foreknown and stable ground rules:

[48] Max Lüthi, *Once Upon A Time: On the Nature of Fairy Tales*, Lee Chadeayne and Paul Gottwald, transl., Frederick Ungar, New York, 1970, p. 24.

[49] William Morris, "The Legend of 'Briar Rose,'" 1890. This pamphlet, available at the British Museum, contains four quatrains intended to caption the Burne-Jones illustrations, for which the pamphlet itself was intended as an advertisement.

. . . miracles, astonishing and central to legends, are a matter of course in the fairy tale.[50]

[The fairy tale hero] doesn't ponder over the mysterious forces or where his helpers have come from; everything he experiences seems natural to him and he is carried along by this help, which he has earned often without his knowledge.[51]

As W.J.M. Bronzwaer[52] has argued about the affect* of verb tense in narrative, once ground rules are established, the major affects arise from "microcontextual" variation, from the local affect of reading at any given time. Although the World of Enchantment is more fantastic than the world of Achebe or Schuyler, it is still a stable world that does not produce continuing astonishment and that does not reverse its own ground rules. *Alice*, on the other hand, does.

Quite early in *Alice in Wonderland*, just as soon as we've gotten used to the flip-flops of the ground rules, and perhaps made a rule of the flip-flops themselves, we get a flop-flip:

Soon her eye fell on a little glass box that was lying under the table: she opened it, and found in it a very small cake, on which the words "EAT ME" were beautifully marked in currants. . . .

She ate a little bit, and said anxiously to herself "Which way? Which way?" holding her hand on the top of her head to feel which way it was growing; and

---

* *Affect*, as opposed to *effect*, both as substantive and as verb, is used throughout this text to refer to "feeling or emotion as distinguished from cognition," a psychological meaning authorized by the usage article in *The American Heritage Dictionary*.

[50] Lüthi, *Once Upon A Time*, p. 47.

[51] *Ibid.*, p. 142.

[52] W.J.M. Bronzwaer, *Tense in the Novel*, Wolters-Noordhoff, Groningen, 1970, esp. chapter 3.

she was quite surprised to find that she remained the same size. To be sure, this is what generally happens when one eats cake; but Alice had got so much into the way of expecting nothing but out-of-the-way things to happen, that it seemed quite dull and stupid for life to go on in the common way.

So she set to work, and very soon finished off the cake.[53]

While fairy tales use the World of Enchantment as their location, and are therefore highly fantastic, a true Fantasy such as *Alice* continues to reverse its ground rules time and again. The World of Enchantment offers a "medium" for portraying the "truth of the human heart." That truth resides in Fantasies also, of course, but Fantasies may be generically distinguished from other narratives by this: the very nature of ground rules, how we know things, on what bases we make assumptions, in short, the problem of human knowing infects Fantasies at all levels, in their settings, in their methods, in their characters, in their plots.

A fairy tale appears often to be a Fantasy because it is concerned with diametric opposition:

This mercy and threat is depicted in a number of variations in the Sleeping Beauty fairy tale. The fairies are both a blessing and a curse for the child; the royal palace is for Sleeping Beauty both paradise and prison; the deathlike sleep both a spell cast upon her and a refuge. The hedge of thorns, which can kill but which finally bursts into bloom with magnificent flowers, expresses most vividly this all-pervading polarity of death and resurrection.[54]

[53] Lewis Carroll, *Alice's Adventures in Wonderland*, p. 33.
[54] Lüthi, *Once Upon A Time*, p. 25.

37

Diametric opposition is a potent structure for a symbol system, and, as all lovers of Hawthorne know well, through such diametric oppositions Romance does present human truth. However, opposition is not reversal. In a fairy tale, and in most narratives, no matter where they fall along the scale of the fantastic, the ground rules of the narrative world accommodate paired opposites. In a Fantasy, the opposition is at the level of the ground rules themselves. In this, Fantasy is unique.

Tolkien says that fairy tales can be used for many purposes, and he enumerates some. However,

> there is one proviso: if there is any satire present in the tale, one thing must not be made fun of, the magic itself.[55]

In this regard, fairy tales are directly opposed to such a Fantasy as *Alice*. Not only can we notice the special quality of a Fantasy in the ever-changing ground rules that provide the context for a character's surprise, but we can notice it in the other signals of the fantastic, the narrator's comment and the structural hints of the implied author. We can see both these at work in the following extract from *News From Nowhere*:

> Opposite to [the public buildings] was a wide space of greenery, without any wall or fence of any kind. I looked through the trees and saw beyond them a pillared portico quite familiar to me—no less old a friend, in fact, than the British Museum. It rather took my breath away, amidst all the strange things I had seen.[56]

William Guest's surprise at seeing the familiar reminds us again that the ground rules of this narrative world are forcibly reversed from, among other things, the perspectives

[55] Tolkien, *The Tolkien Reader*, p. 52.
[56] Morris, *News From Nowhere*, p. 42.

foisted by its 1890s grapholect. Further, the historical implications of the British Museum remind us of the inherently fantastic nature of a future-history structure. We share Guest's surprise when he is told of "the great clearance ["of the beastly monuments to fools and knaves"] which took place over a hundred years ago."[57] In a true Fantasy, the fantastic is ever before us.

"The Continuity of Parks" by Julio Cortázar[58] is a true Fantasy. It is worth quoting in its entirety:

He had begun to read the novel a few days before. He had put it down because of some urgent business conferences, opened it again on his way back to the estate by train; he permitted himself a slowly growing interest in the plot, in the characterizations. That afternoon, after writing a letter giving his power of attorney and discussing a matter of joint ownership with the manager of his estate, he returned to the book in the tranquility of his study which looked out upon the park with its oaks. Sprawled in his favorite armchair, its back toward the door—even the possibility of an intrusion would have irritated him, had he thought of it—he let his left hand caress repeatedly the green velvet upholstery and set to reading the final chapters. He remembered effortlessly the names and his mental image of the characters; the novel spread its glamour over him almost at once. He tasted the almost perverse pleasure of disengaging himself line by line from the things around him, and at the same time feeling his head rest comfortably on the green velvet of the chair with its

[57] Ibid., p. 57.

[58] Julio Cortázar, "The Continuity of Parks," from Blow-up and Other Stories, Paul Blackburn, transl., Collier, New York, 1971, pp. 55-56. The story originally appeared in End of the Game and Other Stories, copyright © 1967 by Random House, Inc. It is reprinted here by permission of Pantheon Books, a division of Random House, Inc., and Joan Blackburn.

high back, sensing that the cigarettes rested within reach of his hand, that beyond the great windows the air of afternoon danced under the oak trees in the park. Word by word, licked up by the sordid dilemma of the hero and heroine, letting himself be absorbed to the point where the images settled down and took on color and movement, he was witness to the final encounter in the mountain cabin. The woman arrived first, apprehensive; now the lover came in, his face cut by the backlash of a branch. Admirably, she stanched the blood with her kisses, but he rebuffed her caresses, he had not come to perform again the ceremonies of a secret passion, protected by a world of dry leaves and furtive paths through the forest. The dagger warmed itself against his chest and underneath liberty pounded, hidden close. A lustful, panting dialogue raced down the pages like a rivulet of snakes, and one felt it had all been decided from eternity. Even to those caresses which writhed about the lover's body, as though wishing to keep him there, to dissuade him from it; they sketched abominably the frame of that other body it was necessary to destroy. Nothing had been forgotten: alibis, unforeseen hazards, possible mistakes. From this hour on, each instant had its use minutely assigned. The cold-blooded, twice-gone-over re-examination of the details was barely broken off so that a hand could caress a cheek. It was beginning to get dark.

Not looking at one another now, rigidly fixed upon the task which awaited them, they separated at the cabin door. She was to follow the trail that led north. On the path leading in the opposite direction, he turned for a moment to watch her running, her hair loosened and flying. He ran in turn, crouching among the trees and hedges until, in the yellowish fog of dusk, he could distinguish the avenue of trees which led up to the house. The dogs were not supposed to bark, they did not bark. The estate manager would not be there at this hour, and he was not there. He went up the three porch steps and entered. The woman's words reached him over the thudding of blood in his ears: first a blue chamber, then a hall, then a carpeted stairway. At the top, two doors. No one in the first room, no one in the second. The door of the salon, and then, the knife in hand, the light from the great windows, the high back of an armchair covered in green velvet, the head of the man in the chair reading a novel.

Here the final twist undercuts all stable perspectives. Was the story told by a real man or a fictional man? Even in our memory of it, the ground rules of Cortázar's true Fantasy continued to reverse themselves—and raise questions about the very nature of fiction.

The fantastic is a quality of astonishment that we feel when the ground rules of a narrative world are suddenly made to turn about 180°. We recognize this reversal in the reactions of characters, the statements of narrators, and the implications of structure, all playing on and against our whole experience as people and readers. The fantastic is a potent tool in the hands of an author who wishes to satirize man's world or clarify the inner workings of man's soul. In more or less degree, a whole range of narratives uses the fantastic. And at the far end of this range, we find Fantasy, the genre whose center and concern, whose primary enterprise, is to present and consider the fantastic. But in varying measure, every narrative that uses the fantastic is marked by Fantasy, and offers us a fantastic world. In the remainder of this book, we will examine those worlds.

41

# ❦ II ❧

# The Fantastic and Escape

THE MOST common of the marks by which we recognize a work that has passed through the world of Fantasy is the vision of escape. As the fantastic involves a diametric reversal of the ground rules within a narrative world, a narrative world itself may offer a diametric reversal of the ground rules of the extra-textual world. If those external ground rules are seen as a restraint on the human spirit—be they, for instance, the belief that there is no excitement in life, the belief in the decline of man, the belief in the lawlessness of the universe—then a fantastic reversal that offers a narrative world in which these ground rules are diametrically reversed serves as a much-needed psychological escape. By examining so-called "escape literature" we can see what the fantastic offers by way of solace and what it reveals about man.

Boredom is one of the prisons of the mind. The fantastic offers escape from this prison.

Alice was beginning to get very tired of sitting by her sister on the bank, and of having nothing to do: once or twice she had peeped into the book her sister was reading, but it had no pictures or conversations in it, "and what is the use of a book," thought Alice, "without pictures or conversations?"

So she was considering, in her own mind (as well as she could, for the hot day made her feel very sleepy and stupid), whether the pleasure of making a daisy-chain would be worth the trouble of getting up and picking the daisies, when suddenly a white rabbit with pink eyes ran close by her.

. . . when the Rabbit actually *took a watch out of its waistcoat pocket*, and looked at it, and then hurried on, Alice started to her feet, for it flashed across her mind that she had never before seen a rabbit with either a waistcoat-pocket, or a watch to take out of it, and, burning with curiosity, she ran across the field after it, and was just in time to see it pop down a large rabbit-hole under the hedge.[1]

With that, the adventures in Wonderland begin, and Alice takes her first step toward the diametric underground reversal of the ground rules of the daylight world of Victorian England: her boredom drives Alice into the world of a book chock-full of pictures and conversations. In similar fashion, Norton Juster establishes Milo's central problem as one of boredom: " 'It seems to me that almost everything is a waste of time,' "[2] the boy says, and thus creates the context for the flip-flop into the book in which "what had started as make-believe was now very real."[3] We make believe because we *want* to make believe, to accept belief, to suspend disbelief. We all know that rabbits don't carry watches, but on a hot summer afternoon, wouldn't it be nice to make believe they did? When we accept a world in which the make-believe is real, we participate in the fantastic. This participation is a form of escape.

Conventionally, *escape*, when used of "escape literature," implies a general evasion of responsibilities on the part of

[1] Lewis Carroll, *Alice's Adventures in Wonderland*, in *The Annotated Alice*, Martin Gardner, ed., World Publishing Company, New York, 1960, pp. 25-26. All references to this book and *Through the Looking Glass* are to the Gardner edition.

[2] Norton Juster, *The Phantom Tollbooth*, Random House, New York, 1967 (1961), p. 9.

[3] *Ibid.*, p. 16.

the reader who should, after all, spend his time on "serious literature." This is a pernicious dichotomy that derives from two misconceptions: first, that "seriousness" is better than "escape"; second, that escape is an indiscriminate rejection of order. Both these misconceptions owe something to the Protestant work ethic.

Escape literature includes "adventure stories, detective stories, tales of fantasy,"[4] pornography, westerns, science fiction,* and, when read for pleasure by adults, fairy tales. Escape literature, according to the conventional wisdom, "aims at no higher purpose than amusement." But in the notions of "higher purpose" and of adults reading in a genre "beneath" them, we see that even today we maintain vestiges of the old prescriptive criticism: some kinds of literature are inherently better than other kinds. However, whatever virtues this position may have, it does not help us address questions of the uses of the fantastic.

The escape offered by these popular genres comes from their ability to exchange the confining ground rules of the extra-textual world not for chaos but for a diametrically opposed set of ground rules that define fantastic worlds. In so doing, authors create for us such works as *The Odyssey*, *Oedipus*, and *Metamorphoses*, to name just one each of "adventure stories, detective stories, tales of fantasy." These are not "beneath" anyone, and their escape is just as potent, and derives from precisely the same reconfiguration of ground rules, as *To Hell and Back*, *And Then There Were None*, and *Pinocchio*, respectively. The theme of a work may seem trivial, its characters uninteresting, its conflicts irrelevant,

---

* This class of works will be discussed at length below in "The Fantastic and Genre Criticism."

[4] C. Hugh Holman, *A Handbook to Literature*, Odyssey, Indianapolis, 1972, p. 203.

44

but if it offers escape, it is in that regard structurally akin to some of the world's great literature.

Escape in literature is a fantastic reversal, and therefore not a surrender to chaos. In its mundane uses, escape may be defined as "emerge from restraint; break loose from confinement."[5] In the United States, the only country that calls its prisons *penitent*iaries, escape surely must imply a delinquent evasion of responsibilities. Since prison is an inherently displeasing environment with onerous ground rules, escape comes to mean any change, escape to anywhere. But escape from the prison of the mind is not so easily had. If the restraint is grounded in one's perceptions of oneself or of the nature of the world, mere change is not enough: one needs a compensating change, a diametric reversal. If boredom is the sign of the mind's one-track fixity, then its opposite, excitement, is what we need. Alice descends into Wonderland, not into Morris' Nowhere or Voltaire's garden. Escape, then, is neither inherently frivolous nor inherently unrestrained; we need feel no guilt in reading escape literature. In the literature of the fantastic, escape is the means of exploration of an unknown land, a land which is the underside of the mind of man.

David Lindsay's *A Voyage to Arcturus* (1920) is one of the most soul-wrenching and mind-distorting Fantasies in English. It is a deadly serious book set on Tormance, the only inhabited planet in the system of Arcturus. Thus, the work has been dismissed as escape literature, science fiction, a mere tale of fantasy; but it is hardly trivial:

It was dense night when Maskull awoke from his profound sleep. A wind was blowing against him, gen-

---

[5] *The Random House Dictionary of the English Language*, unabridged edition, New York, 1966.

45

tle but wall-like, such as he had never experienced on earth. He remained sprawling on the ground, as he was unable to lift his body because of its intense weight. A numbing pain, which he could not identify with any region of his frame, acted from now onward as a lower, sympathetic note to all his other sensations. It gnawed away at him continuously; sometimes it embittered and irritated him, at other times he forgot it.

He felt something hard on his forehead. Putting his hand up, he discovered there a fleshy protuberance the size of a small plum, having a cavity in the middle, of which he could not feel the bottom. Then he also became aware of a large knob on each side of his neck, an inch below the ear.

From the region of his heart, a tentacle had budded. It was as long as his arm, but thin, like whipcord, and soft and flexible.

As soon as he thoroughly realized the significance of these new organs, his heart began to pump. Whatever might, or might not, be their use, they proved one thing —that he was in a new world.[6]

On this fantastic planet, Maskull visits numerous environments, and in each he is physiologically transformed. In this first stage, he is equipped with three new types of organs. The one on his forehead is called a breve. Lindsay also creates for his planet two new primary colors, jale (which creates a soft impression) and ulfire (which conveys wildness as red conveys passion).

Maskull became interested in a new phenomenon. The jale-colored blossoms of a crystal bush were emitting mental waves, which with his breve he could clear-

[6] David Lindsay, *A Voyage to Arcturus*, Ballantine, New York, 1973 (1920), pp. 44-45.

ly distinguish. They cried out silently, "To me To me!" While he looked, a flying worm guided itself through the air to one of these blossoms and began to suck its nectar. The floral cry immediately ceased.[7]

Each new organ gives Maskull, and thus the reader, access to a new mode of perception; each fantastic creature gives us a new perspective on the chain of life. Here "escape literature" is serious indeed. The murders and turmoils, as well as the sexual passions, of Tormance give Lindsay's escape a quality that haunts one long after the reading is over.

Maskull, like Alice and Milo, enters his fantastic world out of boredom. The first chapter gives us a séance designed to jolt the ennui of the worldly Edwardians by exposing them to the otherwordly. Maskull and his friend Nightspore are present at this séance when a materialization occurs during which a dark character named Krag rushes in, strangles the apparition (which dies with a hideous grin on its face), and proceeds to make small talk with our two principals. The special flavor of Maskull's boredom, unlike that of, say, Alice, is a moral immobility. He hardly notices the apparent murder (though later we find that, fantastically, it is himself who was murdered!). Krag and Nightspore, who know each other, talk in the street about the strange world of Tormance.

> [Maskull] asked himself for the first time if this fantastic conversation could by any chance refer to real things. . . . "For twenty-four hours on that Arcturian planet, I would give my life."[8]

Later—many insights, many physiological changes, many environments later—Maskull is asked why he came to Tor-

[7] *Ibid.*, p. 65.     [8] *Ibid.*, p. 26.

mance. " 'To meet with new experiences, perhaps. The old ones no longer interested me.' "9

Although Maskull may make this voyage merely to overcome boredom, we follow him to overcome his specific brand of moral boredom. Tormance is precisely the reconfigured world to give us a compensating moral perspective. Joiwind, a loving woman who acclimatizes Maskull to Tormance's "gravity" by giving him of her own clear blood through symbolic arm wounds that "touch lips" together, explains the rationale for the strangeness of her native place:

> "Life on a new planet, Maskull, is necessarily energetic and lawless, and not sedate and imitative. Nature is still fluid—not yet rigid—and matter is plastic. The will forks and sports incessantly, and thus no two creatures are alike."10

And, as Maskull muses:

> "I am on a strange planet . . . where the very laws of morality may be different."11

Tormance is revealed as a fantastic environment, a map of the underside of man's mind, the hidden world where a morality worn smooth by the repetition of an ordered life maintains yet its crags and sharp edges. These edges stand out in harsh relief in the five-colored light of Arcturus.

Maskull's journey is indeed escape, but fantastic escape, and therefore a constant reminder of the world diametrically escaped from. The fantastic here, as in satire, is a teaching device. The dark message that emerges from Lindsay's book, after Maskull's odyssey, and even after his death and metamorphosis into his Doppelgänger Nightspore, is a message of existential nihilism that stands starkly against

---

9 *Ibid.*, p. 251.  10 *Ibid.*, p. 65.  11 *Ibid.*, p. 91.

the promises of western religion: "the whole world of will was doomed to eternal anguish in order that one Being might feel joy."[12] This is escape literature, but this is not frivolous. "You came . . . to give a deeper life to men—never doubting if your soul could endure that burning."[13]

Of course, not all escape literature has so serious a purpose as *A Voyage to Arcturus*. Pornography, for example, indulges the fantasy that sexual fulfillment comes easily and without the onus of emotional involvement. For this reason even such relatively sophisticated literary works as John Cleland's *Fanny Hill* (1747) follow an essentially episodic structure. Here the escape is to a world, the near opposite of our own, in which there are no entanglements, and hence few of those interweaving strands that knit up the totality of organic art. Perhaps the absurd proof of this is *Naked Came the Stranger* (1969), a novel held together by a woman's decision to sexually destroy as many men as she can. At the same time that Gilly rapes her episodic cohorts, one cohort to a chapter, she rapes our minds by stirring our own prurience. This novel appeared over the name of Penelope Ashe, but that is a pseudonym masking the identities of twenty-six writers for *Newsday*, who "collaborated" on the book, about two writers to each chapter. The interconnections among chapters are so tenuous that Gilly's hair color changes twice with no one's noticing. And, for the engaged reader participating in this minimal escape, the hair color makes no difference. This is escape literature without serious purpose.

However, not all pornography need be without seriousness. Interestingly, there may be a direct correlation between serious purpose in escape literature and the degree of the fantastic. *Sex Sorceress*[14] is what one might call a

---

[12] *Ibid.*, p. 286.     [13] *Ibid.*, p. 152.
[14] Janie Tarlow, *Sex Sorceress*, Spade Publishing, New York, 1969.

"cheap novel." "Every Spade publication is guaranteed to be a genuine manuscript." In this story, an old lecher runs an antique store as a front while making his real money, and sexual contacts, by supplying high school girls with contraceptives, abortions, rin-no-tams, and other assorted oddments. The major plot device is a magic mirror, presumably once belonging to Lucrezia Borgia, that involves the viewer more sensuously than any mirror ever could and reflects not the person's face but his fondest sexual fantasies. The lecher intends using this device to achieve his purposes with the town's one "high breasted" hold-out. The story is, of course, weak. One would even want to call it "pure escapism." And yet, the telling device of the magic mirror (shades of "Snow White"!) has a two-fold effect: it makes the story considerably more fantastic, and it involves the story much more pointedly in the exploration of the human unconscious. Even when attempting "mere" escape, when literature employs the fantastic, it is likely to cast unexpected light on our lives.

With the partial exception of *Sex Sorceress* and other overtly fantastic variants, pornography's escape arises not so much from the anti-expected as the highly dis-expected. Although in normal life an easy liaison is unusual, and a series of a dozen in a week is stretching probability considerably, no fictional series of sexual encounters of itself contradicts possibility. Horror fiction, on the other hand, in its creation of supernatural or otherworldly terrors, contradicts possibility quite often. In this sense in which horror fiction is more radically fantasic than pornography, it is both more radically escapist and more radically revealing.

A paradigmatic example of horror fiction is Poe's "The Black Cat" (1843). The crazed narrator begins his story by admitting, quite sanely, its insanity. "For the most wild yet homely narrative which I am about to pen, I neither expect nor solicit belief." Indeed, we may come to see the events as "nothing more than an ordinary succession of very natural causes and effects."[15] The narrator tells how he deterioriated under the influence of alcohol. In the course of his degradation, the last humane feeling to erode was his love of animals, especially his large black cat Pluto (note the portentous name). Finally, still drinking, he one day "hung it *because* I knew that in so doing I was committing a sin." God too seems to recognize this sin, because coincidentally the narrator's house catches fire. He flees the house, but returns the next morning.

> . . . the head of my bed. The plastering had here . . . been recently spread. About this wall a dense crowd were collected, and many persons seemed to be examining a particular portion of it with very minute and eager attention. The words "strange!" "singular!" and other similar expressions, excited my curiosity. I approached and saw, as if graven in *bas-relief* upon the white surface, the figure of a gigantic *cat*. The impression was given with an accuracy truly marvelous. There was a rope about the animal's neck.[16]

This report is central to the narrator's sense of horror, horror not so much at his crime but at his impending punishment. He takes this portraiture for a supernatural portent, and the reports of himself and the crowd agree in signalling the fantastic. In the real world, one drowns cats with impunity; in this tale of fantastic horror, retribution will work its inexorable course.

The impression of control from above is further strength-

[15] Edgar Allan Poe, "The Black Cat," in *The Complete Tales and Poems of Edgar Allan Poe*, Hervey Allen, ed., Modern Library, New York, 1938, p. 223.
[16] *Ibid.*, p. 225.

ened by the narrator's discovery of another black cat in, appropriately, a saloon. This cat follows the narrator home. The man tolerates the cat though he quickly develops an "absolute *dread* of the beast." This second cat is identical to Pluto save that it has a single white marking:

> The reader will remember that this mark, although large, had been originally very indefinite; but, by slow degrees—degrees nearly imperceptible, and which for a long time my reason struggled to reject as fanciful— it had, at length, assumed a rigorous distinctness of outline. It was now the representation of an object that I shudder to name—and for this, above all, I loathed, and dreaded, and would have rid myself of the mon- ster *had I dared*—it was now, I say, the image of a hideous—of a ghastly thing—of the *Gallows!*—oh, mournful and terrible engine of Horror and of Crime —of Agony and of Death![17]

We now see clearly that the narrator's idea of crime is not doing evil to others but suffering retribution against him- self. It comes as no surprise that he finally does try to dis- patch the cat. But his long-suffering wife interferes. From the narrator's perspective, it is quite reasonable that, though the description of the gallows portraiture was quite long, the following is short indeed:

> Goaded by the interference into a rage more than de- monical, I withdrew my arm from her grasp and buried the axe in her brain. She fell dead upon the spot without a groan.[18]

The narrator proceeds to hide the body by walling it up in the cellar "as the monks of the Middle Ages are recorded

[17] *Ibid.*, p. 227.          [18] *Ibid.*, p. 228.

to have walled up their victims." Finishing the job, he notices that the cat is missing. Bewilderment. Joy. And two days pass. Blessed relief. But finally the inevitable: the police have been called by the neighbors because they haven't seen the wife lately. Our narrator personally takes them through the house, watches tensely as they examine the floor and walls of the basement, and becomes more relaxed and finally cocky as he sees that they can find nothing. As they are about to leave, he brags about the sound construction of his home and

> through the mere frenzy of bravado, I rapped heavily with a cane which I held in my hand, upon that very portion of the brickwork behind which stood the corpse of the wife of my bosom.
>
> But may God shield and deliver me from the fangs of the Arch-Fiend![19]

he continues, for the blow calls forth "one long, loud, and continuous scream." The police break down the wall and discover the corpse, and, perched on its head, the black cat.

Thus, in Poe's story, the facade of the rational coats every occurrence, yet the signals of the fantastic let us know how we must take the tale: God lives, it seems; certainly some consistent law wreaks justice in this narrative world. It is by this law that we see the archfiend as the narrator himself, man his own worst enemy, and see that this archfiend grows with alcohol and perverts fellow feeling. Although in the extra-textual world guilt often goes unpunished, in this "escape" literature we know from the very first fantastic portraiture that guilt will be punished. This is an ordered world, a world that, despite its horror, gives us faith. And lest it be objected that the faith is groundless, because the po-

[19] *Ibid.*, p. 230.

lice do not always get their man, it must be remembered that the story's deeper meaning is that the man will always get himself, an insight for most of us into the underside of human psychology. In horror fiction such as Poe's, precisely because it is fantastic, we find that the escape leads us to the truth of the human heart.

"The Black Cat" proceeds, from fantastic occurrence to fantastic occurrence, to a final confirmation of the beliefs we adopt quite early in the story. In a sense, our memory of the first page serves as a prediction of the last, and when the last page is read, we read it not as a surprise, but as a confirmation devoutly to be wished. This process of reading in a fantastic landscape reinforces the White Queen's assertion that "it's a poor sort of memory that only works backward."[20]

The genre for which we have the most detailed account of the processes of forward memory is also one of the most fantastic genres: the fairy tale. In *The Morphology of the Folktale* (equivalent to fairy tale according to the translator), Vladimir Propp develops a powerful hypothesis:

Tales possess one special characteristic: components of one tale can, without any alteration whatsoever, be transferred to another.[21]

Propp is saying that *all* fairy tales are structurally alike. First he defines "function."

Function is understood as an act of a character, defined from the point of view of its significance for the course of the action.

[20] Lewis Carroll, *Through the Looking Glass*, p. 248.
[21] Vladimir Propp, *Morphology of the Folktale*, Laurence Scott, transl., University of Texas Press, Austin, 1968, p. 7.

Propp then expresses his general conclusion in four theorems:

1. Functions of characters serve as stable, constant elements in a tale, independent of how and by whom they are fulfilled. They constitute the fundamental components of a tale.
2. The number of functions known to the fairy tale is limited.
3. The sequence of functions is always identical.
4. All fairy tales are of one type in regard to their structure.[22]

The exhaustive demonstration of Propp's thesis takes many volumes, his own merely the first in a long series of cross-cultural studies that have tested these conclusions, and, so far, found them valid.[23] What we can take from this study without the demonstrations, however, is the notion that in a genre that is well defined, and therefore comes to the reader with a host of structural predictions, forward memory—anticipation based on past acquaintance with the genre—must work strongly.

Propp manages to specify his second theorem by listing thirty-one functions and their variants. Some of these are obligatory (they must occur), some optional, but whichever *do* occur, they always occur, according to the third theorem, in their numerical order. From this, the fourth theorem follows logically. Even with Grimm tales, which

[22] *Ibid.*, pp. 21-23.
[23] There are some minor discrepancies that emerge in testing Propp's theories. For example, some functions may freely be trebled, according to Propp. That is, instead of the hero having to answer one testing riddle, he may have to answer three. In Amerind cultures, where things come not in threes but in fours, trebling functions quadruple. The discrepancy is clearly not serious.

are removed from their folk sources, we can see these functions arise in their normal order. Following are Propp's first five functions and my own paraphrase of the beginning of "Red Riding Hood":

I. One of the members of a family absents himself from home.
II. An interdiction is addressed to the hero.
III. The interdiction is violated.
IV. The villain makes an attempt at reconnaissance.
V. The villain receives information about his victim.[24]

I. Red Riding Hood is sent to bring food to Grandmother, who lives in the forest.
II. Red Riding Hood is told not to tarry in the forest.
III. She stops to chat with the wolf.
IV. The wolf asks where Red Riding Hood is going.
V. She reveals the location of Grandmother's cottage.[25]

In similar fashion, "Red Riding Hood" proceeds to fulfill the expectations of our forward memories step by step according to the functions first described by Propp but known from time immemorial to the unconscious of the world.

The fairy tale world is a controlled world. Max Lüthi points out that "The Fairy tale conquers time by ignoring it."[26] He might have pointed out with equal force that the fairy tale conquers chaos by ignoring it also. He does note that the style of the fairy tale operates by a kind of clarity

---

[24] Propp, *Morphology*, pp. 26-28.

[25] ———, "Red Riding Hood," from "*Seven Fairy Tales* by The Brothers Grimm," in *Once Upon A Time: The Fairy Tale World of Arthur Rackham*, Margery Darrell, ed., Viking, New York, 1972, p. 55.

[26] Max Lüthi, *Once Upon A Time: On the Nature of Fairy Tales*, Lee Chadeayne and Paul Gottwald, transl., Frederick Ungar, New York, 1970, p. 44.

that is the diametric reversal of the shades and nuances of the extra-textual world:

> Its individual stylistic features are in harmony with each other; they aim for clarity, exactness, positiveness, and precision. . . . Every fairy tale is, in its own way, something of a dragon slayer.[27]

Further, Lüthi asserts that children need the cruelty (which is described with crystalline sharpness, never bloody gore) of grim fairy tales in order to learn, by seeing danger handled safely and symbolically, that their own fears can be mastered.[28]

Thus, by the structure that Propp describes and the style that Lüthi describes, we find that the simple "Once upon a time" convention launches us immediately into a highly specified fantastic world. This world is an escape from our own, but, as with Poe, an escape through a diametric, fantastic reversal, so that the narrative world actually explores the underside of our conscious world. This world of escape is a controlled world, controlled not by the archfiend within us but by the conventions of the fantastic genre itself. Where we had always sensed disorder, suddenly we see there can be order.

Red Riding Hood gets to her grandmother's house, goes through the famous three exchanges with the wolf (what big eyes, hands, and teeth) and is eaten. A huntsman hears the wolf snoring loudly in the cottage (how these villains give themselves away by their own gluttony!) and investigates to see if the old woman is all right. He is about to shoot the wolf but "it just occurred to him that perhaps the wolf had eaten up the old lady, and that she might still be saved."[29] He takes out his knife, opens the beast, and (fan-

---

[27] *Ibid.*, p. 57.  [28] *Ibid.*, p. 113.
[29] ———, "Red Riding Hood," p. 56.

tastically) out pops Red Riding Hood and then Grandmother. Once liberated by the knife ("it was so dark inside
the Wolf!"),

> Red Riding Hood brought some big stones with which
> they filled the Wolf, so that when he woke and tried to
> spring away, they dragged him back, and he fell down
> dead.
> They were all quite happy now. The Huntsman
> skinned the Wolf, and took the skin home. The Grand-
> mother ate the cake and drank the wine which Red
> Riding Hood had brought, and she soon felt quite
> strong. Red Riding Hood thought: "I will never again
> wander off into the forest as long as I live, if my
> Mother forbids it."[30]

The intrinsic structural orderliness of the fairy tale world
cooperates here with a style dependent on some fairly obvious symbolism to bring home the reassuring message that
woman's sexuality is, after all, worth the trouble. The day
is saved by the penetrating knife of the huntsman (who rejects his own destructive weapon, the gun). Once the knife
cuts open the dark "belly" in which the females are trapped,
the young, fecund girl (she has received the mantle of
menses, the Red Hood, from her grandmother) brings
earthy matter to kill the wolf herself (though presumably
the gun is still available), makes possible the huntsman's
pursuing his occupation, and rejuvenates the grandmother
with food. The dark forest in which the wolf has tempted
her to tarry by directing her eyes to "the sunlight dancing
through the trees, and all the bright flowers"[31] is the forest
of sensual pleasure. Red Riding Hood's experience has
taught her not to tarry there, but only because, for a girl
still struggling with the onset of sexuality, the time is too
soon. The last phrase of the story looks toward a future time

---

[30] *Ibid.*, p. 58.    [31] *Ibid.*, pp. 55-56.

when Red Riding Hood's mother, and the mother of the child hearing the story, will no longer forbid a sojourn in the forest.[32]

In both "Red Riding Hood" and "Briar Rose," we have seen that a fantastic world, a world apparently offering escape from our own, really speaks directly to us. By making a fantastic reversal of the rules of our world and offering an ordered world, fears of maturation can be met and symbolically tamed. This quite serious purpose of escape literature is accomplished by a well defined and highly predictive structure in cooperation with a conventional and stable style that signals the presence of that structure. A key feature of both structure and style is the interdiction (or sometimes prophecy): a statement early on in the story that just has to come true by the end. The story creates an ordered narrative world in which such convenient coincidence feels believable. This sense of knowable regularity, evident in different ways in both horror fiction and fairy tales, is the distinguishing mark of perhaps the most popular class of escape literature: detective fiction.

W. H. Auden writes that

the fantasy . . . which the detective story addict indulges is the fantasy of being restored to the Garden of Eden, to a state of innocence.[33]

---

[32] One should note that this type of analysis may be widely applied to fairy tales if one considers not only the content of the tale but the probable audience. In the Grimm version of "Red Riding Hood," the moral acts as a gentle restraint on budding sexuality, both a caution and a promise. In Perrault's version of the story, the little girl is devoured and not saved; the moral is much more cautionary and holds little promise. Clearly that tale would transmit values of a less sexually free culture than those of the Grimm version, or perhaps transmit values felt appropriate for a younger, and hence further from marriage-age, audience.

[33] W. H. Auden, *The Dyer's Hand and Other Essays*, Random House, New York, 1948, p. 158.

This is a soothing, rejuvenating fantasy, a compensation for an excess of the chaos of the world. After the criminal and unjust denouement of *The Great Gatsby*, for instance, Nick Carraway returns to the West, the perennial place of rebirth for the American Adam:

> When I came back from the East last autumn I felt that I wanted the world to be in uniform and at a sort of moral attention forever.[34]

The military metaphor is an apt one: Nick wants control from above; he wants a world of knowable regularity in which justice is done; he wants a fairy tale world, an escape world, a fantastic world. In *The Warlord of the Air*, Moorcock's character Ulianov (Lenin) uses the innocence component of Auden's and Fitzgerald's Garden metaphor:

> "A revolutionist is a man who, perhaps, fails to keep his innocence but so desperately wants it back that he seeks to create a world where all shall be innocent in that way."[35]

We all lose our innocence sometime. Few of us become revolutionists; many of us read detective fiction.

We can perhaps best locate the defining characteristics of the genre of detective fiction by examining a range of its most famous examples: Edgar Allan Poe's "The Purloined Letter" (1845), Arthur Conan Doyle's "The Speckled Band" (1892), and G. K. Chesterton's "The Blue Cross" (1911).* We will find, with slight variation, that these stories share a number of features: they appear to be explicitly fantastic;

---

* In "The Fantastic and Literary History" below we will consider dectective fiction more broadly from Poe to the present.

[34] F. Scott Fitzgerald, *The Great Gatsby*, Charles Scribner's Sons, New York, 1953 (1925), p. 2.

[35] Michael Moorcock, *The Warlord of the Air*, Ace Books, New York, 1971, p. 174.

this fantastic quality is naturalized by explanation within a stable set of ground rules; the explanation immediately follows an action that either brings justice or reasserts the morally right; both the explanation and the action are accomplished by the detective, a man of intellect and high seriousness; the detective's success is predictable within the known ground rules of the narrative world; the nature of the success is actually prophesied. Thus, at the end of the tale, the prophecy is fulfilled and order is reestablished. The great detective's appeal is parallel to Prospero's then,[36] and the time spent in Dupin's Paris or Holmes' London is much like time spent on the "Bermoothes." Knowing that the world is orderly can be a great consolation.

"The Purloined Letter" begins with the narrator, the nameless reader's friend, sitting with his comrade, C. Auguste Dupin. The narrator muses on their many successes as they share a silent "Meerschaum." Enter the Prefect of Police. He says he will want advice, strictly out of curiosity, about an affair which is "so simple, and yet baffles us altogether." Dupin responds with his prophecy: " 'Perhaps the mystery is a little *too* plain.' "[37] The Prefect launches into a lengthy tale: Minister D., an able but unscrupulous man, has purloined a letter that can be used as blackmail against a "certain party," clearly a mistress of the King. It is further known that the letter must be handy to be effective, and therefore must be in D.'s house or on his person. Conveniently, D. is of regular habits, and the police

[36] An interesting treatment of Prospero as the paradigm for the superior, controlling force in a fictive world can be found in Robert Plank, *The Emotional Significance of Imaginary Beings*, Chas. C. Thomas, Springfield, Illinois, 1968, esp. chapter 6. Plank's ultimate conclusion is that all such figures, from Sherlock Holmes to Wells' invading Martians, fascinate us because their actions resonate with our own experience of the Oedipus complex.

[37] Edgar Allan Poe, "The Purloined Letter," p. 209.

have used his walks to waylay him twice, as if by thieves, to search him; they have spent a full week probing the furniture and false drawers of each room in D.'s apartments. " 'Then,' " the narrator says, reflecting the thoughts of an ordinary man, " 'you have been making a miscalculation, and the letter is *not* upon the premises, as you suppose.' "[38] Dupin, though, admits no such thing. He asks for a description of the document, which the Prefect gives, and the interview is over.

"In about a month afterward [the Prefect] paid us another visit, and found us occupied very nearly as before."[39] We see developing here in the early stages of the genre a recurrence of the Renaissance notion of *sprezzatura*. According to this ideal, an accomplished courtier could dash off a poem, defend his honor, or play at love, all with an expertise marked by the off-hand manner of one working beneath his capacities. Many courtiers worked quite hard at effortlessness. By the nineteenth century, the modern myth of the Renaissance Man was established, and this myth infects the characterization of the modern omni-capable hero, the detective. Dupin, like the later Holmes and Father Brown, is never rushed, always prepared, and ever calmly in control.

On this second occasion, Dupin and the Prefect fence verbally, each ignoring the question of the letter. Finally Dupin brings up the subject and wonders how much the lady in question would pay for its return. The Prefect will not say, but says, "I wouldn't mind giving my individual check for fifty thousand francs to any one who could obtain me that letter." Dupin is not satisfied with mere willingness, however, and finally extracts a promise.

[38] *Ibid.,* p. 213.
[39] *Ibid.*

"I would *really* give fifty thousand francs to anyone who could aid me in the matter."

"In that case," replied Dupin, opening a drawer, and producing a checkbook, "you may as well fill me up a check for the amount mentioned. When you have signed it, I will hand you the letter."

I was astounded. The Prefect appeared absolutely thunder-stricken. For some minutes he remained speechless and motionless, looking incredulously at my friend with open mouth, and eyes that seemed starting from their sockets. [The Prefect writes the check; Dupin hands over the letter.] This functionary grasped it in a perfect agony of joy, opened it with a trembling hand, cast a rapid glance at its contents, and then, scrambling and struggling to the door, rushed at length unceremoniously from the room and from the house, without having uttered a syllable since Dupin had requested him to fill up the check.

When he had gone, my friend entered into some explanations.[40]

These explanations take the remaining 60 percent of the tale.

Poe's narrative strategy is quite simple here, and quite effective. The first half of the story establishes firmly, by the Prefect's exposition of the problem, that the letter is impossible to obtain. In a rapid interchange the impossible is diametrically reversed, not only made possible, but made actual. The signals of the fantastic are rife in this passage: the narrator's astonishment, the Prefect's speechlessness. But the fantastic is then naturalized. It was possible to create the thrill of the fantastic by establishing one set of ground

[40] *Ibid.*, p. 214.

rules, but at a less conscious level, the dominating presence of Dupin, his own reticence, the prophecy, and even the introductory reminiscences have created a deeper belief that the fantastic is excluded from this world. Though the thrill of the fantastic may function microcontextually, in the larger tale the ground rules are stable. As Dupin says, " 'I dispute the availability, and thus the value, of that reason which is cultivated in any special form other than the abstractly logical.' "[41] Poe's task in the second portion of the story is to prove that Dupin's miraculous materialization was indeed a natural occurrence.

Dupin, it is explained, proceeds first to "an identification of the reasoner's intellect with that of his opponent."[42] (This is a common trick of fictional great detectives and consequently a common habit of mind for devotees of detective fiction. In Agatha Christie's *The A. B. C. Murders* [1936], for instance, after everyone is satisfied that the killer is behind bars, Poirot thinks on: " 'The case is ended! The case! The case is the *man*, Hastings. Until we know all about the man, the mystery is as deep as ever.' ")[43] Dupin explains how his own attempt at this identification must be superior to that of the Prefect, a man trained in the methodical procedures of the police:

> . . . had the principle of its concealment been comprehended within the principles of the Prefect—its discovery would have been a matter altogether beyond question. This functionary, however, has been thoroughly mystified; and the remote source of his defeat lies in the supposition that the Minister is a fool, because he has acquired renown as a poet.[44]

[41] *Ibid.*, p. 217    [42] *Ibid.*, p. 215.
[43] Agatha Christie, *The A. B. C. Murders*, Dodd, Mead, New York, 1936, p. 255.
[44] Poe, "The Purloined Letter," p. 217.

Science and art are often seen as antagonistic. Poe himself makes this point in his 1829 sonnet "To Science." The man of science alone may be a fallible drudge (like the Prefect) or a mad scientist (kin to Faust or, at this period, Hawthorne's overreaching scientists such as Rappaccini or Aylmer of "The Birthmark"), but the Great Detective, the modern Prospero, a Renaissance Man, can accommodate both science and art (recall Holmes' violin playing, for example, or Nero Wolfe's horticulture). In this accommodation, the detective does not turn back logic but finds a higher logic. Since, as Dupin reasons, the Minister would be well aware of the police methods for dealing with the complex art of concealment, "he would be driven, as a matter of course, to *simplicity*."[45] The tale naturalizes the fantastic by revealing that there has been indeed a direct reversal, but not a reversal of the ground rules themselves. ". . . to conceal his letter, the Minister had resorted to the comprehensive and sagacious expedient of not attempting to conceal it at all."[46]

Dupin then put his theory to the test. He visited the Minister, spotted the letter and, on a second visit, switched it for a decoy. Thus, not only has the letter been returned, but the Minister is unaware of the return. This is an important point, because now the previously compromised lady, rather than being at the mercy of the Minister's superior evidence, is herself in a position made superior by her knowledge. Although the Minister believes he has a damning letter, the lady knows he does not. She can play brinkmanship to the very hilt.

The whole tale up to this point has proceeded, with one minor but significant exception, as if the only matter really at hand were the solution of a puzzle. Indeed, in explaining his reasoning to the narrator (and thus to the reader),

[45] *Ibid.*, p. 219.   [46] *Ibid.*, p. 220.

Dupin analogizes his mental process to the strategy behind "a game of puzzles . . . played upon a map"[47] in which one is required to pick out place names. While the inexperienced player demands that his opponent find names in minute lettering, the experienced player will demand those names writ large across the whole map.

As Thomas Kuhn points out about the normal scientist's mania for solving puzzles, "though intrinsic value is no criterion for a puzzle, the assured existence of a solution is."[48] The engagement with a puzzle is the engagement with a form. The prophecy, the dominance of the intelligence in control of the rules, these guarantee that the detective story is formally soluble, and therefore offers the pleasures of a puzzle. In the extra-textual world, except in normal science, only such problems as are manufactured for the purpose have guaranteed solutions: a puzzle is a toy; it offers us escape into a world in which solutions are guaranteed. Detective fiction offers us, by naturalizing the fantastic, the same escape.[49]

However, detective fiction can provide us with another escape, the escape into the world of justice, the world in which the *problem* of evil becomes only the *puzzle* of evil, and the sufficiently skilled detective can always bring the world to "a sort of moral attention." The minor exception to Poe's purely formal exposition was the slight hint of hu-

---

[47] *Ibid.*, p. 219.

[48] Thomas S. Kuhn, *The Structure of Scientific Revolutions*, University of Chicago Press, Chicago, 1970 (1962), p. 37.

[49] In Agatha Christie, *Murder in the Calais Coach* (orig. *Murder on the Orient Express*), Dodd, Mead, New York, 1934 (Pocket Books, New York, 1974), M. Bouc, a friend of Poirot, says of the mystery in which they are involved, " 'The whole thing is a fantasy' " (p. 124). Nonetheless, because Bouc has turned over the investigation to the great detective, he feels justified in demanding that Poirot " 'Show me how the impossible can be possible' " (p. 119). (Page references to Pocket Book edition.)

man characterization: the Minister is capable but unscrupulous. From the Enlightenment on, the man of science has been an ambivalent figure, sometimes lauded (Pasteur), sometimes vilified (Victor Frankenstein). "There are some things that man was not meant to know" reminds us that there is a moral order in the world. Dupin restores that order.

The narrator asks Dupin why he troubled to plant a decoy letter instead of merely taking the genuine one; in either case, the reward check would have been forthcoming. Dupin then explains how the decoy letter confers power on the lady, and so, like a chivalrous, jousting knight, he not only vanquishes evil, but puts it at the mercy of good.

> "In the present instance I have no sympathy—at least no pity—for him who descends. He [the Minister] is that *monstrum horrendum*, an unprincipled man of genius."[50]

The evil by science created is by science laid to rest. Poe's Dupin stories offer us an escape into a world in which we needn't fear that might makes right, for the highest might, as in the medieval trials by combat, resides always with the man of right. The detective rules a world that offers us, by taming the fantastic, both the escape of the puzzle and the escape of justice.

Holmes too offers us both escapes. Professor Moriarty is the best remembered symbol of evil in Doyle's works, but each of the stories has such a symbol. In one of the most famous, "The Speckled Band," we learn early on that Dr. Grimesby Roylott is the murderer. The puzzle in this story requires figuring out how Roylott managed the deed in a room locked from the inside by the victim; the dispensation of justice depends upon the solution coming quickly enough

[50] Poe, "The Purloined Letter," p. 222.

to save the next prospect, the victim's sister. Holmes, of course, manages both. By deduction, later confirmed by observation, Holmes realizes that a snake must have been trained to enter a ventilator hole, crawl down a bell rope, and then bite the occupant of the bed near which the rope hangs. Having first safely sent the sister away, Holmes is able to wait patiently for the snake, which he beats with a cane, sending it scurrying back to Dr. Roylott's room where it kills the would-be killer. Puzzle solved; justice restored; moral science conquers evil scientist (doctor).

Just as in fairy tales, the rescue comes in the nick of time. The fantastic death in a locked room is naturalized.

In the very beginning of the tale, Watson defines the narrative world. Like Dupin, Holmes was

> working . . . rather for the love of his art than for the acquirement of wealth . . . [consequently] he refused to associate himself with any investigation which did not tend towards the unusual, and even the fantastic.[51]

Holmes' mode of deduction is a paradigm of the fantastic naturalized: first he amazes his hearer by revealing unknowable information, then he further amazes the hearer by showing that his information was logically knowable after all. In this tale, Holmes is brought into the case by the anxious sister, Helen Stoner. She knocks on the famous door at 221B Baker Street and the gentlemanly detective asks her to come in and be seated. She is trembling with fear.

> "You must not fear," said he soothingly, bending forward and patting her forearm. "We shall soon set matters right, I have no doubt. You have come in by train this morning, I see."

[51] Arthur Conan Doyle, "The Adventure of the Speckled Band," in *The Complete Sherlock Holmes*, Doubleday, Garden City, New York, 1930, vol. I, p. 257.

"You know me, then?"

"No, but I observe the second half of a return ticket in the palm of your left glove. You must have started early, and yet you had a good drive in a dog-cart, along heavy roads, before you reached the station."

The lady gave a violent start and stared in bewilderment at my companion.

"There is no mystery, my dear madam," said he, smiling. "The left arm of your jacket is spattered with mud in no less than seven places. The marks are perfectly fresh. There is no vehicle save a dog-cart which throws up mud in that way, and then only when you sit on the left-hand side of the driver."

"Whatever your reasons may be, you are perfectly correct."[52]

Holmes' world is a fantastic world, but a fantastic world naturalized. Holmes could, should he choose to, abandon his books just as Faust tried too late to do and as Prospero did quite in time to restore normalcy and justice. Like Prospero, Holmes tries to teach others the secrets of his power, but the secrets are beyond them. And like Miranda, Helen Stoner doesn't care because, not only as puzzler, but as justicer, Holmes is trustworthy:

"I have heard, Mr. Holmes, that you can see deeply into the manifold wickedness of the human heart. You may advise me how to walk amid the dangers which encompass me."[53]

Holmes is indeed an omni-capable Renaissance Man, even more so than Dupin. Where Dupin is clever, Holmes is both clever and strong. Note the *sprezzatura* and self-restraint with which Holmes responds to the threats of Dr. Roylott:

[52] *Ibid.*, pp. 258-259.    [53] *Ibid.*

"I am a dangerous man to fall foul of! See here." He stepped swiftly forward, seized the poker, and bent it into a curve with his huge brown hands.

"See that you keep yourself out of my grip," he snarled, and hurling the twisted poker into the fireplace he strode out of the room.

"He seems a very amiable person," said Holmes, laughing. "I am not quite so bulky, but if he had remained I might have shown him that my grip was not much more feeble than his own." As he spoke he picked up the steel poker and, with a sudden effort, straightened it out again.[54]

In Holmes' enchanted world, the prophecy is somewhat reduced. In Helen Stoner's report of her sister's death, she notes that the sister collapsed and uttered these final words: "Oh, my God! Helen! It was the band! The speckled band!"[55] We know what to look for, yet certain false clues (a gypsy band on Roylott's grounds, for instance) put us off the track. But Holmes knows. Without having revealed his ratiocination to Watson or the reader, he has sent Helen away and stationed himself in her bedroom with Dr. Watson, the drudge man of science akin to the Prefect. When Holmes hears the hiss, he strikes a previously prepared match and by its light lashes out with his cane. The light goes out. Seconds later, there is a scream from Dr. Roylott's communicating bedroom. The detectives rush in and Watson notices "Round his brow he had a peculiar yellow band. . . . 'The band! the speckled band!' whispered Holmes."[56] The prophecy is fulfilled. In fact, the band is a snake that has bitten and killed the doctor. In the final paragraph, Holmes asserts that "my cane roused its snakish temper . . . [which was] responsible for Dr. Grimesby Roylott's

[54] *Ibid.*, p. 265.    [55] *Ibid.*, p. 262.    [56] *Ibid.*, p. 272.

death"[57] In this way, the prophecy comes true on many levels: the speckled band revealed as a snake not only solves the puzzle, but the snake's killing Roylott restores justice and frees the damsel from fear. The "snakish temper" reference implies that, as in "The Black Cat," the villain is killed in large measure by his own evilness. It is no accident that one writer established the formulae for both the horror tale and the detective story.

Like "The Purloined Letter," "The Speckled Band" is both a puzzle and a moral tale. In the development from Poe to Doyle we see the same basic pattern of detective fiction, but with a shift in emphasis: the puzzle quality becomes somewhat less important, the moral quality becomes somewhat more important. In Chesterton, that development toward morality continues.

"The Blue Cross," the first of the Father Brown series, is the story of how an arch criminal named Flambeau can lead a poor priest astray. On the criminal's trail the whole time is Aristide Valentin, the great French detective. Flambeau, Valentin knows, has overheard Father Brown on the train:

> He explained with a moon-calf simplicity to everybody in the carriage that he had to be careful, because he had something made of real silver "with blue stones" in one of his brown-paper parcels.[58]

Most of the story recounts how Valentin follows the clues he alone can pick out because of his superior identification with the intellect of the criminal. Just as Flambeau is about to attack the little cleric on Hampstead Heath, Valentin shows up to arrest the thief. Valentin wonders how the priest could have gone off with Flambeau without suspicion,

[57] *Ibid.*, p. 273.
[58] G. K. Chesterton, "The Blue Cross," in *Stories, Essays and Poems*, Everyman, London, 1965, p. 5.

71

especially since the criminal had tried to pass himself off as a fellow priest. But Father Brown explains that he had been in control of the situation continuously: the clues were left not by Flambeau but, fantastically, by mild Father Brown himself, because he knew that a policeman like Valentin would assume the clues had been left by the criminal; the cross with blue stones, in fact, had already been safely posted to its destination; and Brown knew all along that Flambeau was no priest because "he attacked reason. . . . It's bad theology."[59] In other words, by appearing simple, Father Brown had been able to create a highly complex puzzle for Valentin, Flambeau, and the reader. Father Brown had been master of his world all along. "I saved the cross, as the cross will always be saved."[60] Where justice had been a side benefit of puzzle-solving in Poe, puzzle-solving in Chesterton has become a tool in the service of justice.

Of our three authors, Chesterton takes belief in moral right furthest of all.

> The most incredible thing about miracles is that they happen. A few clouds in heaven do come together into the staring shape of one human eye. . . . Nelson does die in the instant of victory; and a man named Williams does quite accidentally murder a man named Williamson. . . . In short, there is an element of elfin coincidence which people reckoning on the prosaic may perpetually miss. As it has been well expressed in the paradox of Poe, wisdom should reckon on the unforeseen.[61]

To reckon on the unforeseen is to participate in the fantastic. Maskull says, " 'Nothing turns out as one expects.' "[62]

[59] *Ibid.*, p. 23.    [60] *Ibid.*    [61] *Ibid.*, p. 6.
[62] Lindsay, *A Voyage to Arcturus*, p. 242.

Chesterton has taken the classic detective tale, noted its fantastic roots in the elfin escape of the fairy tale, and remade it. Instead of using the tale to ease maturing, as the Grimm brothers did, instead of using the detective tale to calm the fear of science as Poe and Doyle did, Chesterton uses the real-world implications of the fantastic world to reaffirm the existence of a higher order. Chesterton wants the escape world of the detective narrative to become our actual world.

In some fashion, escape literature always presents the reader with a world secretly yearned for. If that world is merely the too-good-to-be-hoped-for accumulation of the dis-expected, as in pornography, it may reveal much about the writer and/or reader, but will not serve to give either a new perspective on the mental constraints from which they seek escape. However, if the escape world is based on a fantastic reversal, then, as with the fairy tale, that escape need not be a descent into triviality but a message of psychological consolation. Fantasy is not random freedom from restraint, but the continuing diametric reversal of the ground rules within a narrative world. When escape literature is not random but is rather the establishment of a narrative world that offers a diametric reversal of the ground rules of the extra-textual world, then escape literature is to an important degree fantastic, and, for its audience, psychologically useful. If we know the world to which a reader escapes, then we know the world from which he comes.

# ❦ III ❧

# The Fantastic and Perspective

It is not easy to know the world from which a reader, or a writer, comes. That world is made of a vast number of perspectives, angles of vision, modes of apprehending. To one person, the exact opposite of *man* may be *woman*; to another, the opposite of *man* may be *boy*. The difference is one of perspective. We can learn about perspective by studying the extra-textual circumstances of an utterance or by asking people to reveal their own preoccupations. But at the same time, we can more easily locate those preoccupations, define those perspectives, if we know what a person takes to be operative oppositions. As we have seen, fantastic literature, be it literature of escape, fairy tale, or true Fantasy, is founded on the structural inclusion of diametric opposition; and as we have also seen, we can often locate the fantastic reversal by purely intra-textual signals. The study of the fantastic, then, may serve as a fully coequal complement to the study of the normative in arriving at a sense of the perspectives of readers and writers. The study of the fantastic provides new tools for the analysis of world-view.

It has been recently demonstrated that the "prevalence of a particular genre of swearword generally relates to cultural taboos." This means that the escape offered by iconoclasm, an escape that may be signalled by tone of voice, can help us locate the taboos themselves in a culture. More specifically, a second study indicates that people who occupy repetitive jobs, jobs we today call "dehumanizing" and per-

74

haps even confining, use swearwords as 24 percent of their utterances, while people in professional, perhaps less confining, jobs use an amazingly low 1 percent.[1] Not only can we locate a society's taboos by noting its swearwords, but by studying the frequency and distribution of swearwords, the junctures at which escape seems both needed and possible, we can define the relation of components of that society to those taboos. When the fantastic Peter Pan rejects maturity in favor of childhood, we know that a failure to shoulder responsibilities is an iconoclastic assault on the Victorian perspective toward personal achievement; when we find that Barrie's book is ostensibly directed to children, we know something more about both the Victorian conception of childhood and the means by which iconoclasm—escape —may be made acceptable; and when we realize that all those best-selling copies of the book were bought by adults and read to children by adults, we know something further about the yearnings of normal Victorian adults. In their children's Fantasies are revealed their own perspectives.

Of course, one must also know the normative in order to properly locate the fantastic. In a true Fantasy we find the repeated reversal of the ground rules of the narrative world. When this reversal is structural, as in Cortázar's "Continuity of Parks," we know we have implicitly located the normative perspectives on fiction by their particular reversals. However, the idea that fictional characters are not real is so widespread a perspective that alone it tells us little. Individual reversals in the establishment of a fantastic world may be more helpful.

We all know that the dead, like flowers, don't speak. And yet perhaps they do, according to the perspective of a given

[1] ———, *Time*, 20 May 1974, p. 73. The article adduces studies by psychologists Vladimir Piskacek and Paul Cameron as well the *The Anatomy of Swearing* by Ashley Montagu.

speaker. At the beginning of a television newscast,[2] the reporter said:

Edward Kennedy "Duke" Ellington died this morning
of cancer of the lungs and pneumonia. Later in the program we'll hear him play for us.

That this utterance was not intended to astonish seems clear
from the context of the program and the respectful tone of
the speaker; this was not to be taken as a fantastic reversal
of the ground rules of some particular world. If the language (dialect or grapholect) of the 1970s carries with it
the perspectives of electronic storage and retrieval of
music, then by that language a previously fantastic notion
has been naturalized. Nonetheless, the imputation of Ellington's teleology, "we'll hear him play *for us*," for a group
made up now of the reporter and his hearers, that imputation should still be fantastic. Yet to the reporter it wasn't.
Seen from the reporter's perspective, Ellington's music was
alive and still audience-directed; the announcer had faith
in the miracle of his medium. His world, like that of a fairy
tale, might well be seen as fantastic, but he was operating
wholly within that world, and so his utterances were not
fantastic at all. His unconscious retreat into the fantastic
world of electronics, a retreat made easy by his occupation,
offered consolation by a process quite akin to that whereby
the detective story offers consolation. In this case, death was
conquered in a presumably objective newscast. This process
is revealed to us, and the detailed perspectives of a given
time and place are revealed to us, through the complementary study of the normative and the fantastic.

Edmund Carpenter points out that

[2] John Chancellor, *NBC Nightly News*, 24 May 1974.

those who find the physical and social environments too demanding, too messy, sometimes seek to live, as far as possible, within media environments.[3]

The retreat is dependent not only on medium, but on different versions of a medium. Supporting the (often-contested) Sapir-Whorf hypothesis, Carpenter assumes that language differences make at least some actual differences in worldview.

> Language does more than label: it defines; it tells not only what a thing is, but also its relation to other things. I may say that this pencil is lying *on* the table, making both pencil & table nouns, separate objects, with *on* indicating their relationship. But a Wintu would say, "The table lumps," or, if there were several things on the table, "The table lumps severally." The Wintu and I experience different realities, not simply the same reality in different ways.[4]

Many linguists find this assertion of different "realities," as opposed to different "ways," quite troubling. Perhaps the apparent disagreement can be sidestepped, however, at least for the purposes of literary argument. If we grant the primacy of perception[5] (as the phenomenologists do), then perhaps we can view the difference between "realities" and "ways" as one asserted more for rhetorical effect than for substance. Probably neither party in this linguistic debate would disagree that our controlling visions are often

[3] Edmund Carpenter, *Oh, What a Blow That Phantom Gave Me!* Holt, Rinehart and Winston, New York, 1972, p. 10.

[4] *Ibid.*, p. 19.

[5] See Maurice Merleau-Ponty, "The Primacy of Perception," in *The Primacy of Perception and Other Essays*, Northwestern University Press, 1964, for an argument in support of this position based on firm aesthetic grounds.

adopted unconsciously; nor would either party quarrel with the notion that our controlling visions—our perspectives— are reflected in our language. Let us ignore the question of the existence of a world beyond our perceptions and, since we are studying the perceived phenomena of literature, confine ourselves to those literary perceptions. These surely, as Carpenter asserts, vary with linguistic differences.

Use of a particular language generates large-scale differences that only affect us consciously when we work in a bilingual context. But linguistic variations of controlling vision impinge on us unconsciously every time we read or talk. If English implies perspectives that to some extent oppose those of Wintu, then we can reasonably expect the grapholect of 1850 English to carry with it at least some perspectives about electronic media that oppose those associated with the grapholect of 1970 English. Continuing to focus this notion, and adopting Barthes' terminology for the description of language, there should exist, even within a single grapholect (*écriture*), variations of perspective that correlate with style, and, more particularly, variations of perspective that correlate with individual texts. Most specifically, when linguistic perspectives continually shift within a given text, that is, when the ground rules of the narrative world are subjected to repeated reversal, we have Fantasy. Our modes of analysis of the fantastic, then, should be applicable to a wide range of problems in the definition and comparison of worldviews.

Carpenter asserts that language is the defining component of one's sense of reality,[6] and in making this assertion he discusses what he calls "symbols." Kenneth Burke, taking a more flexible position, sees "Perspective as Metaphor."

[6] Carpenter, *Oh, What a Blow*, p. 17.

78

The heuristic value of scientific analogies is quite like the surprise of metaphor. The difference seems to be that the scientific analogy is more patiently pursued, being employed to inform an entire work or movement, where the poet uses his metaphor for a glimpse only. (Yet even here we may find a similarity; the complete works of the poet show signs of a unified attitude precisely such as may be summed up in one metaphor: "He calls life a dream . . . or a pilgrimage . . . a carnival . . . or a labyrinth.")[7]

To this suggestion we can add others. Many works seem to distill their constellation of perspectives into a single metaphor, often the title character. *Peter Pan* is again an example.[8] By a close analysis of metaphor, by attention to all language used to create a fantastic world, we can discover the alternative perspectives of a writer, or, by extension, his culture. Knowing these alternative perspectives, we can infer the normative perspectives from which they offer fantastic escape. Using this information in the type of complementary study we have already suggested, we should be able to refine and reconfirm our sense of any particular worldview.

Worldviews themselves, of course, are subject to drastic change; they respond to the society around them. Indeed, some might say they define the society that adopts them. Noel Perrin is able to give us an example of a remarkably complete reversal of perspective within a single lifetime:

[7] Kenneth Burke, *Permanence and Change*, Bobbs-Merrill, Indianapolis, 1965 (1954, 1935), p. 96.

[8] The distillation of perspective into a single metaphor is a feature of works with a romantic structure, and, though not frequent, is widespread; note the centrality of the daemon to *Frankenstein*, Dublin to *Dubliners*, or Cash McCall to the novel of that title. The relationship of central metaphor to the diachronic structure of ro-

79

When [Walter Scott] was about twenty-one, in the 1790's, one of his great-aunts wrote him saying that she was short of reading matter, and asking if he could get hold of the novels of Aphra Behn for her. Scott said yes, he could, if she insisted, but he warned her that she wouldn't like them, as they were improper. The old lady did insist, and Scott mailed them [in plain brown wrappers]. Very soon she mailed them back, having quit early in the first novel. It is "a very odd thing . . . that I, an old woman of eighty and upwards, sitting alone, feel myself ashamed to read a book which, sixty years ago, I have heard read aloud for the amusement of large circles, consisting of the best and most creditable circles in London."[9]

Smut is in the eye of the beholder. It is, in this case, all a matter of perspective.

In order to try out the analytic tools we have been discussing, we might be well served to pick a society and a time that seem fairly stable. Once we learn how to analyze worldview, and its component perspectives, at a given historical moment, we can begin to explore extensions of these methods into the analysis of the historical development of worldviews (see below, "The Fantastic and Literary History"). One period that is likely to serve our purposes well is that of England between, say, 1860 and 1895. Victoria reigned supreme, had been reigning supreme, and would reign supreme. Albert died in 1861 and Victoria's native moral and philosophical constancy was augmented by her constancy to the memory of her husband. She was mother,

---

mance is discussed in Eric S. Rabkin's *Narrative Suspense*, University of Michigan Press, Ann Arbor, 1973, pp. 115-26.

[9] Noel Perrin, *Dr. Bowdler's Legacy, A History of Expurgated Books in England and America*, Macmillan, London, 1970 (1969), p. 9.

even grandmother, to the English and to their steadily growing empire. We may look upon the empire as imperialist, bloody, and exploitative, but the High Victorians saw each military encounter as a skirmish that they underwent nobly in order to uphold their God-given responsibilities: white man's burden. Although slavery had been abolished in the mother country in 1833, the idea of moral superiority played a constant bass as Britannia danced through a full generation of self-congratulatory expansion.

There were problems at this time, of course. Dickens first spread wide the warning against the philosophy of Benthamite utilitarianism and the Industrial Revolution it supported when he published *Hard Times* (1854). Perhaps the worst assault on the English way of life came not from her traditional enemies (who were busy carving out empires of their own and recuperating from a series of revolutions and political reshufflings that centered around the years 1820, 1848, and 1870), but from competition with the United States. Though ravaged by the Civil War, the United States bounced back: 1866, second transatlantic cable; 1869, Union Pacific Railroad; 1870, Standard Oil Company. With communication, transportation, and fuel availability all multiplied enormously, the Great Plains became not only the breadbasket of Chicago and New York, but of London and Manchester. The greatest social upheaval of this placid High Victorian generation was the destruction of British Agriculture in the 1870s.[10] The consequence of this trade assault, unlike the consequences of the political shifts when Scott was young and the French were declaring a Republic, was not a redefinition of society, but an intensification of its problems. The cities became fuller, the country emptier, the machine shops sweatier, the beggars dirtier. Although the

[10] G. M. Trevelyan, *Illustrated English Social History*, volume 4, Longmans, Green, London, 1952, p. 91.

British may have felt themselves to be upholding the white man's burden, they were just as surely seeking foreign markets for their manufactured wares. As Winston Churchill said just before the Great War rolled over that "right little, tight little Island": "The maxim of the British people is 'Business as usual.'" On 13 November 1887 a large body of unemployed marched peacefully in Trafalgar Square to protest their condition. They had been refused a parade permit. The police in overwhelming numbers charged the marchers and two died. William Morris was one of the leaders of this march. "Bloody Sunday" convinced him that revolution was impossible in England. To a Victorian, times may have been troubled, but the order of things was fixed: history proceeded inexorably toward its civilizing goal.

In this generation from 1860 to 1895, High Victorianism rested on a tripartite base. The first leg was a particular perspective on history, and this perspective led to fantastic escapes in the works of William Morris (1834-1896). The second leg was a particular perspective on religion, and George MacDonald (1824-1905) offered by far the most popular and enduring alternative to that. The third leg, perhaps the leg that stands yet and balances the precarious structure of our own society, was a particular view of science. C. L. Dodgson (1832-1898), writing under the name of Lewis Carroll, created the most pointed and enduring alternative to that perspective. Most writers, of course, combined these three perspectives both in mapping out normative fictional landscapes and in inventing fantastic ones. These three fantasists themselves each touch on all three perspectives; but in their works the concern with one perspective clearly overshadows concern with either of the others. Each of these writers was enormously popular in his own day, and each is still deemed worthy of attention now. A study of the life, times, and works of these men argues strongly that the special worldview of the High Victorian era was the result of a special confluence of perspectives on history, religion, and science.

William Morris,[11] only after the Queen herself, is perhaps the best exemplar of the age of Victorianism. His accomplishments are legion. Son of a stockbroker, growing up beside Epping Forest but with daily ties to the commercial focus of the City, he was already in his youth a child of his ambivalent times. He went up to Oxford, but, instead of completing his education, became articled to an architect, an obligation he was able to free himself from in order to join Ruskin, the Rossettis, and other Pre-Raphaelites-to-be in the mural decoration of the Oxford Union (1857). He was an accomplished painter, but throughout his life he preferred "architecture," by which he meant an approach to art that sees art as enveloping man, forming his total environment. At the Victoria and Albert Museum, that great repository of crafts, furniture, fashions, and *objets d'art*, the William Morris Company decorated an entire room, with Morris himself responsible in whole or part for the wallpaper designs and production, the furniture design and production, the decoration of the cabinetry (which included pictures of Arthurian subjects), the design of the silverware, the design and production of the stained glass windows, the carpeting, everything. No other designer in England's history was offered such a commission.

Morris not only worked in wood and oil and paper and glass, but he worked in history. The techniques of glass staining had been lost and through his researches these were regained. Indeed, despite the canard that Morris hated machinery, he modernized and improved these lost techniques, as he also improved by use of modern ma-

[11] The best life of Morris is Philip Henderson, *William Morris*, Thames & Hudson, London, 1967.

83

chinery the techniques of wallpaper printing, woodcut printing, and tapestry making, an art that again he alone retrieved. Although there was a folk model in his mind when he designed it, it is fitting that the Morris chair bear the name of the firm that made it well known. This firm, a financial success, produced all these items Morris dealt in, either directly or by supplying designs and specifications and supervision to subcontractors. He said, "Have nothing in your home which you do not know to be useful or believe to be beautiful," and he created a full range of items to fill that requirement.

This omni-disciplinary production was one manifestation of Morris' ideal of life as an integrated whole. He manifested this aim in many ways. He had two tests for the desirability of a new machine: first, would it produce goods more cheaply without lowering utilitarian or artistic quality; second, would the workman who must employ the machine find the activity of using it rewarding. If a machine met these standards, Morris was only too eager to adopt it, manufacture useful art with it, and turn a tidy profit. His employees worked either on a profit-sharing basis, or, if paid wages, were paid at above the going standards. What Robert Owen attempted at New Lanark Mills with an insufficient financial base, Morris accomplished, albeit with fewer workers, at Merton Abbey.

In his family life alone can one see Morris falling short of his ideals. His hauntingly beautiful wife Jane carried on a long-time liaison with Dante Gabriel Rossetti, one of Morris' closest friends and co-workers. Morris seems never to have tried actively to prevent their meeting, nor does he seem to have taken up any such affairs himself. He viewed the whole matter with a combination of sadness and gnawing failure; his compensation for these feelings came through his work, his writing, and his life as a public man.

In the political realm, Morris was one of the most important propagandists of the nineteenth century. In 1877, he founded Anti-Scrape (the Society for the Protection of Ancient Buildings), which did more than any other group to keep England's architectural heritage alive. He cofounded and frequently taught at the London Trades Guild of Learning, an early—and successful—experiment in workingman's education. But perhaps most important, after the internal turmoil of the Socialist League, which he had joined in 1883, he founded in 1884 its most potent successor, the Hammersmith Socialist Society. One can get some idea of the centrality of this group to English reform thinking by considering that at its lectures Shaw and the Fabians began their own political education, while Marx's brilliant daughter Eleanor was glad to serve as secretary during Morris' presidency. The house organ of this group was *Commonweal*, long a powerful voice in political affairs. Besides writing some two thousand pamphlets on art and politics, Morris also edited *Commonweal* until 1890. In that year, he published serially the century's most thorough utopian romance, *News From Nowhere*.

To all these accomplishments, one must add Morris' attainments as a man of letters. His first book of verse, *The Defence of Guenevere* (1858), was well received; and his retelling of famous myths, *The Earthly Paradise* (1868-1870), enjoyed good sales throughout the century. He published popular verse translations of Vergil (1875) and Homer (1887). As he had re-found glass staining, he re-found saga literature when he learned Icelandic and made England's northern tradition available for the first time. *Sigurd the Volsung* (1876) is perhaps Morris' best translation from the Icelandic; it is still the standard translation of this particular cycle. Indeed, his poetic accomplishments were sufficiently great that when Tennyson died after having presided over a generation as Poet Laureate (1850-1892), the post was offered to Morris (who declined what he viewed as a controlled position). The last years of his life were devoted to prose, and in them he produced voluminously: *The Well At The World's End, The Sundering Flood, The Water of the Wondrous Isles, The Wood Beyond the World.* These he not only wrote, but published. He founded Kelmscott Press in 1890 and there designed, printed, and bound the books that were to return book design to an art and set a standard of excellence that has never been displaced. Many authorities still consider the Kelmscott Chaucer, produced in the year of Morris' death, to be the finest book ever made. For it, Morris designed ornamental borders and initials and a complete new font. His lifetime friend, Sir Edward Burne-Jones, designed the graphics. For both, it was a labor of the love of letters. In his press, in his writing, in his business, in his politics, in his art, in his teaching, William Morris, by every Victorian measure, was a success. His own ideal was that of an integrated life and perhaps no modern man has ever achieved such an ideal so completely. And yet he wanted to escape. The Prologue to *The Earthly Paradise* begins with these lines:

> Forget six counties overhung with smoke,
> Forget the snorting steam and piston stroke,
> Forget the spreading of the hideous town;
> Think rather of the pack-horse and the down,
> And dream of London, small, and white, and clean,
> The clear Thames bordered by its gardens green. . . . [12]

This is an escape not merely from a nasty present, but an escape from a view of history, a view that sees man shackled to an inexorable, mechanical struggle. Morris is often

[12] William Morris, *A Choice of William Morris's Verse*, Geoffrey Grigson, ed., Faber and Faber, London, 1969, p. 97.

seen as anti-technological, but his only fear is that technology represents a view of the linear progress of history.
It was Marx who made popular the notion of history as a
locomotive; history technological, linear, progressing, inhuman. Marx was a revolutionist, and what he sought was
a garden, Moorcock's innocence, and he assumed it would
come because he shared the Victorian faith in the coming
golden age. As political man, Morris too made this assumption. But as a whole man, he did not.

Tennyson's lines most quoted in his own time express well
the Victorian faith in "expansion about a central stability."[13]

> Let knowledge grow from more to more,
> But more of reverence in us dwell;
> That mind and soul, according well,
> May make one music as before,
> But vaster.[14]

Although Tennyson's *Idylls* are Arthurian, they never offer
their settings as escape so much as a pretty locale for re-
viewing what to the Victorians were contemporary moral
problems, especially problems of religious faith and sexual
freedom. The Victorians measured the world by their own
shadows. Even though it was Dickens who gave us our first
anti-industrial novel, he too loved the locomotive, loved its
daring speed, and unconsciously saw it as the symbol of a
progress that was good. In a letter to John Forster he wrote:

> [Turin] is a remarkably agreeable place. The contrast
> this part of Italy presents to the rest is amazing. Beauti-
> fully made railroads, admirably managed; cheerful,
> active people, spirit, energy, life, progress.[15]

[13] Trevelyan, *Illustrated Social History*, p. 105.
[14] Alfred Tennyson, quoted in Trevelyan, *ibid.*, p. 104.
[15] Charles Dickens, quoted in Herbert L. Sussman, *Victorians and
the Machine*, Harvard University Press, Cambridge, Mass., 1968, p. 47.

This railroad society was just the one Morris asked his readers to "forget." He was right to refuse Tennyson's mantle.

Herbert L. Sussman, not specifically intending the special meaning of *escape* as directly reversing alternative to a given perspective, nonetheless places Morris' fictional writings well in using that term:

> . . . the symbol of the machine formed the essential rhetorical link between the Marxist and Ruskinian elements in Morris' social criticism, [but] it had no place in his poetry. His imaginative writing is quite frankly escapist . . . he found its moral justification in its providing his readers with a similar escape from the mechanized world.[16]

Yeats called Morris "the happiest of poets," and said that the twelve lines beginning "Golden Wings" (from *The Defence of Guenevere*, 1858) were the best description of happiness he knew:[17]

> Midways of a walled garden,
>     In the happy poplar land,
>     Did an ancient castle stand,
> With an old knight for a warden.

> Many scarlet bricks there were
>     In its walls, and old grey stone;
>     Over which red apples shone
> At the right time of the year.

> On the bricks the green moss grew,
>     Yellow lichen on the stone,
>     Over which red apples shone;
> Little war that castle knew.[18]

[16] Sussman, *ibid.*, p. 126.
[17] William Butler Yeats, "The Happiest of Poets" (1902), in *Essays and Introductions*, Macmillan, London, 1961, p. 60.
[18] Morris, *Choice*, pp. 69-70.

We can see how this landscape might well be seen as a geographic correlative for happiness. It is drawn in elementary colors (scarlet, red, green, yellow) and recalls images from a romanticized medieval past, a time when life was integrated, times were not "out of joint," and everything happened "at the right time of year." The moss reveals an unhurried culture, while the "grey stone" reveals a stable, changeless one. It is a "walled garden," but unlike postlapsarian Eden, we are on the inside. There is not a scrap of metal to be seen. We are off the rails of history.

What Sussman forgets in calling this "frankly escapist," and what Yeats forgets in calling this "happy," is that there is as much more to the poem as there was more to the poet. The story of "Golden Wings" is the story of a maid who, in the midst of this Camelot setting, is unhappy because she wants a knight of her own. She sings a song and calls for "Gold wings across the sea!" She cannot wait, however, watching every other character disport with pleasure (they have such Arthurian names as Isabeau and Gervaise), so she commits suicide. This is the only reported act in the poem, yet because of it the people of this narrative world "must meet the war." In lines inverting those Yeats loved, the poem ends:

> The apples now grow green and sour
> Upon the mouldering castle-wall,
> Before they ripen there they fall:
> There are no banners on the tower.
>
> The draggled swans most eagerly eat
> The green weeds trailing in the moat;
> Inside the rotting leaky boat
> You see a slain man's stiffen'd feet.[19]

Time has started up, because of human longing, and time has brought disorder and decay. The movement of history

[19] *Ibid.,* p. 77.

is inimical to the world of the opening lines, and Morris already early in his career laments that he cannot, even in poetry, escape the locomotive of history.

The notion that time brings decay, that history is leading toward ruin and springs from female sexuality, is at the heart of this volume of poems. The title poem has Guenevere defending her own sexual activities to Gawain, and in the second poem, "King Arthur's Tomb," she kisses Lancelot over the displayed corpse of her husband as the era of Camelot crumbles around them. This is the dark side of the Eden myth; to desire escape from such a view puts one in the company of Milton. Morris, however, did not believe in God. He believed in people.

If the sagas serve in part as an escape[20] for Morris from the Victorian perspective of history as linear progress, his own prose romances serve this end entirely. *The Wood Beyond the World* (1894) is such a work. Merely a glance at the title page transports one "beyond the world." The borders, the type face, the graphic woodcut of the fecund virgin, all these are by Morris, put together, printed, and published by him at his own Kelmscott Press. Using a pseudo-medieval grapholect and nearly invoking the conventional formulae of fairy tale, the text begins:

A while ago there was a young man dwelling in a great and goodly city by the sea which had to name Langton on Holm. He was but of five and twenty winters, a fair-faced man, yellow-haired, tall and strong. . . .[21]

[20] "To both Morris and Yeats, Icelandic and Irish saga offered a mode of escape from the pressure of reality. They created from it a land of romantic mirage where the values of reality do not enter." Dorothy M. Hoare, *The Works of Morris and Yeats in Relation to Early Saga Literature*, Cambridge University Press, Cambridge, 1937, p. 141.

[21] William Morris, *The Wood Beyond the World*, Dover, New York, 1972 (facsimile of orig. 1894 Kelmscott Press edition), p. 1.

This fair-haired lad is "winters" old, not "summers" old, because his life so far has been blighted. Although the tale proceeds with the kennings ("rock-wall" for "mountain") and twisted syntax of a presumably magic time, "Golden Walter" is oppressed by a not-at-all magical problem: he has a faithless wife. Unlike Victorian man, however, he has someplace to run. In the course of his runnings, he sees visions of "a maid, a mistress, and a dwarf." His father's trusted servant comes to retrieve Walter, because the father has died, but they are shipwrecked on a strange shore. Here they meet the first of many characters who are in their stations because they have either attacked or been faithless to their fathers.

Walter, rather than proceed homeward, goes over the mountains. This is an example of the Hyperborea myth, an ancient myth much employed by the Victorians, which posits an innocent, uncorrupted people in a pristine land of milk and honey over the last range and beyond the north wind. In Morris' version, though, the Hyperborean land turns out to be an enchanted world under the malevolent control of the envisioned mistress, a beautiful witch who holds the maid in servitude and whose evil errands are performed with relish by the dwarf. After much sparring and testing and frank sexuality, Walter and the maid run off.

This maid is a virgin. Like Miranda, she is unaware of her own beauty. She tells Walter that she overheard him apostrophizing her:

> Then she reddened sorely, and said: I knew not that aught of me had such beauty as thou didst bewail.[22]

She has extraordinary powers (like virgins who were thought the only people able to capture unicorns) exempli-

[22] *Ibid.*, p. 227.

fied by a rejuvenating conceit that Yeats singled out for praise:

> Lo then! as she spake, the faded flowers that hung about her gathered life and grew fresh again; the woodbine round her neck & her sleek shoulders knit itself together and embraced her freshly, and cast its scent about her face. The lilies that girded her loins lifted up their heads, and the gold of their tassles fell upon her . . . the eglantine found its blooms again, and then began to shed the leaves thereof upon her feet; the meadow-sweet wreathed amongst it made clear the sweetness of her legs.[23]

By this power of restrained and magical sexuality, she establishes herself as the god of the savage bear-folk, and thus saves her own life and Walter's, but

> Now shall I tell thee . . . did I not before? . . . that while I am a maid untouched, my wisdom, and somedeal of might, abideth with me, and only so long.[24]

Since Walter and the maid long to marry, and since it wouldn't be safe to remain with the bear-folk after the maid had lost her god-head, the couple leave this part of the wood beyond the world and come through another mountain pass into a land named for its capital city, Stark-wall. Walter is made king of this land because his coming fulfills the requirements for a new king given by the creation myth of the natives,[25] and so he safely takes the maid to wife and queen (having forgotten entirely—and presumably justifiably—about his first wife). The maid is a maid no longer.

In this tale, unlike the poems of *The Defence of Guenevere*, love can lead to happiness and time can proceed without decay. We can divide concepts of time into three gross

---

[23] *Ibid.*, p. 215.  [24] *Ibid.*, p. 229.  [25] *Ibid.*, p. 243.

types: mythic time (time out of time, eternity stretching endlessly in all directions, changeless), aevum (the time of the angels, a time that begins at some known point, such as the creation of the world, but proceeds forever after), and history (time bound fore and aft by events, time that comes in discrete units).[26] History can be further seen as linear and progressive (as the Victorians generally did), as a repetitive cycle (as the Hellenes did), as a progressive spiral (as Yeats did), and so on. In the true wood beyond the world, in the land under the witch's curse, we are in a narrative world that functions, as do fairy tales, in mythic time. However, once the maid loses her virginity, we move into the aevum. She regrets having fooled the bear-folk into thinking her a god and, though queen of Stark-wall, returns to bring them agriculture. Her coming starts the process of change within stability (the aevum) for the culture of the bear-folk. Then she returns to Stark-wall, where Walter is king and she is powerless (having used her sexuality merely to start the historicizing process), and we have history.

But history is precisely that perspective Morris and so many Victorians found confining. He could hardly argue that history was not linear and progressive—his whole life was the perfect confirmation of that Victorian view. Instead, Morris distances history beyond the gulf of a disconnected and impassable historical gap, and thus creates a history in a fairy land so that we can escape into a history that is demonstrably not progressive because it is not connected with our own times. In the ending of the tale, Morris reminds us that myth is the time of Hyperborea; that society can then be created there and so events can happen in it that are not repeatable; that this leads to history; but

---

[26] A brilliant discussion of the relation of man's senses of time to his engagement with fictional form is Frank Kermode, *The Sense of an Ending*, Oxford University Press, New York, 1966.

this history can be a safe and pristine record of a past with which we are not connected:

> Now of Walter and the Maid is no more to be told, saving that they begat between them goodly sons and fair daughters; whereof came a great lineage in Stark-wall; which lineage was so strong, & endured so long a while, that by then it had died out, folk had clean forgotten their ancient custom of king-making; so that after Walter of Langton there was never another king that came down to them poor & lonely from out of the Mountains of the Bears.[27]

In this *Wood Beyond the World*, the reader finds a self-contained escape from the Victorian perspective on history. The story is one of female sexuality bringing one through the stages of myth, aevum, and history, but done in such a way as to create a history wholly independent from our own. Morris creates an alternative to, an escape from, the Victorian perspective on history.

Morris wrote for adults. Serious Victorians were happy to indulge in romantic glances at the Middle Ages, as they did in Tennyson's *Idylls* and Morris' own *Guenevere*, but the less historically justified and more fantastic escape offered by *The Wood Beyond the World*, that was something else. When Walter has his first vision of the mistress, the maid, and the dwarf, he sees them boarding a ship:

> . . . at first he was minded to go ask shipmaster Geoffrey of what he knew concerning the said ship and her alien way-farers; but then it came into his mind, that all this was but an imagination or dream of the day, & that he were best to leave it untold to any.[28]

[27] Morris, *The Wood Beyond the World*, p. 260.
[28] *Ibid.*, pp. 8-9.

Plainly, Walter would not admit to "imagination" because he feared scorn. "Imagination" in Victorian England was for children. In *News From Nowhere*, set in a future in which the most approbative comment is "like the fourteenth century," Old Hammond is explaining life and the then-utopian present to his grandson Dick and the narrator/inquisitor William Guest:

> "How is it that we find the dreadful times of the past so interesting to us—in pictures and poetry?"
>
> . . .
>
> "It is the child-like part of us that produces works of imagination. When we are children time passes so slow with us that we seem to have time for everything. . . . At least let us rejoice that we have got back our childhood again. I drink to the days that are!"[29]

Most Fantasies are atavistic, they hearken to an earlier historical era or an earlier personal era; both times are distinguished from the adult present in that they are not progressive times laden with responsibilities and future death. In atavism lies stability, and in atavistic times, imagination may play safely. When Morris no longer feared scorn, he created a fantasy escape into such a pre-historic realm. Most Victorian authors, creating their own escapes, chose instead to seem to be addressing children.

With one author after another of famous children's stories, we find it asserted that the work was first intended for a particular child. This is the case with *Alice in Wonderland* (1865); with Ruskin's only fantasy, *King of the Golden River* (1841); with Kingsley's *Water Babies* (1863); and with the works of such modern authors as Pamela Travers (*Mary Poppins*), A. A. Milne, J.R.R. Tolkien, and C. S.

[29] William Morris, *News From Nowhere*, James Redmond, ed., Routledge & Kegan Paul, London, 1970, pp. 86-87.

Lewis. If the fantastic offers, in part, direct escape from those perspectives necessary to function in the adult world, then it is perhaps understandable that conceiving of one's proper audience as a child makes one more able to seriously postulate a diametric alternative to those very perspectives that create in us the need to escape.

In *On Aggression*, Konrad Lorenz discusses animal behavior, but his study is suggestive of further reasons for the special liberating powers associated with a child audience. He asserts that

. . . sacred custom owes its motivating force to phylogenetically evolved behavior patterns of which two are of particular importance . . . militant enthusiasm by which any group defends its own social norms and rites against another group not possessing them; . . . the group's cruel taunting of any of its members who fail to conform with the accepted "good form" of behavior.[30]

In other words, people who don't adopt our perspectives will be made members of an outgroup, they will have sanctions brought against them, they will lose standing. Children have not yet learned "good form," and consequently constitute such an outgroup.

Lorenz tells how the aggressive rejection of one's own species works among turkeys. If a turkey hen is sitting on her own eggs and any other turkey comes by, she will peck at it as hard as she can. Even after the eggs are hatched, the chicks stay near her and she pecks anything resembling a turkey that is not so large as to cause her to flee entirely. However, a question arises: why doesn't the turkey hen attack her own chicks? It was discovered that turkey chicks

[30] Konrad Lorenz, *On Aggression*, Marjorie Kerr Wilson, transl., Harcourt, Brace & World, New York, 1966 (1963), pp. 258-259.

96

have a phylogenetically determined behavior pattern they retain until they are sufficiently large to leave the nest: they cheep incessantly. Turkey hens will not attack their own chicks and, when another hen's chicks are introduced into the nest, they too will escape attack. However, if the hen's eardrums are punctured, she will immediately begin to peck to death every chick that fails to flee, both those of other hens and her own.

> The fact that animal mothers of brood-tending species do not attack their young is thus in no way a self-evident law, but has to be ensured in every single species by a special inhibition such as the one we have learned about in the turkey hen.[31]

If a human adult were to spill milk repeatedly at the table of a prim Victorian house, he would be forceably rejected from the group, made an outgroup member, and perhaps abandoned. But a child, if he is too strongly sanctioned, will cry, and that crying, as well as smallness of size, elicits in adult humans certain protective feelings that, if not indulged, lead to guilt and a future coddling of the child. *Homo sapiens* takes longer to raise its young to adult ingroup status than any other species. It is reasonable then that *Homo sapiens* is more strongly geared than any other species to accept outgroup behavior from its young. The perspectives from which adult writers wish to escape are adult perspectives; it is allowable to reverse them in the presence of children.

This freedom of childhood makes children seem somehow blessed. Their wrongs are allowable wrongs, and therefore they may be seen as intuitively wise. Certainly the Victorians felt this. Child wisdom was a wisdom perhaps better than the "knowledge" Tennyson sought.

[31] *Ibid.*, p. 119.

. . . the genius [genie], instead of burdening his pupils with perishable riches and vain sciences, conferred upon them the boon of perpetual childhood. (William Beckford, 1786)

So much superior are the qualities of the Heart to those of the Understanding, that could unsullied Innocence be purchased by the sacrifice of every other consideration, the price would be cheap. (John Bowdler, Jr., 1801)

. . . it is no use trying to account for things in Fairy Land; and one who travels there soon learns to forget the very idea of doing so, and takes everything as it comes; like a child, who, being in a chronic condition of wonder, is surprised at nothing. (George Mac-Donald, 1858)

Come, read my riddle, each good little man;
If you cannot read it, no grown-up folk can.
(Charles Kingsley, 1863)

That children love the book is a very precious thought to me, and, next to their love, I value the sympathy of those who come with a child's heart to what I have tried to write about a child's thoughts. (C. L. Dodgson, 1885)

George MacDonald perhaps more than any other writer of the Victorian era used the strength of the Victorian perspective on children to justify the escape from the Victorian perspective on religion. Among his works are such children's best sellers as *At the Back of the North Wind* (1871), *The Princess and the Goblin* (1872), and *The Princess and Curdie* (1883), works which Auden considers second only to the Alice books as children's literature.[32] Unlike less serious authors, MacDonald allowed his view of children to motivate Fantasies that were clearly intended for adults as well. The best of these, excluding some novellas, were *Phantastes* (1858) and *Lilith* (1895). In all his works, MacDonald uses the allowed Fantasies of childhood to offer true consolation for all ages from the rigors of contemporary religious doctrines.

George MacDonald was a weaver's son, grew up in a happy home, and became a Congregational minister. He was "called to the living" at Arundel in 1850, but by 1853 was forced out under pressure just short of a heresy trial. MacDonald decided to live by his pen and his tongue. He wrote in four genres: children's Fantasies, adults' Fantasies, sermons (both delivered and undelivered), and adventure stories [he was often thought Scott's close second for novels of the Highlands such as *David Elginbrod* (1863) and *Robert Falconer* (1868)]. In addition, his consoling homilies (heretical though they might have been) were frequently gathered in such volumes as *Helps for Weary Souls* (1885) and enjoyed their own brisk sale.[33] (One such is still in print, *George MacDonald: An Anthology*, introduced and edited by MacDonald's most fervent modern reader, C. S. Lewis.) Despite this wide and varied popularity, however, MacDonald, who had a large family, was always in financial need, and so he always wrote. Despite their spiritual consolation and their frequent stylistic brilliance, many may feel that there is just too much of the works of George MacDonald.

[32] W. H. Auden, introduction to George MacDonald, *The Visionary Novels of George MacDonald*, Noonday Press, New York, n.d., p. vi.

[33] See John Malcolm Bulloch, *A Centennial Bibliography of George MacDonald*, Aberdeen, The University Press, 1925, pp. 54ff.

What is too much, however, and what is not enough, is, like so much else, a matter of perspective. George's son Ronald recalls how journalists often noted that his father had thirteen children because he had once written that their number was "the wrong side of a dozen."[34] In fact, MacDonald had eleven children, and the confusion reveals as much about the attitudes of the journalists as it does about MacDonald. In the same way, MacDonald's running skirmish with heresy rests not on some demonstrable fault for a Christian, such as denying the existence of God, but rather on a matter of perspective.

Antinomianism is

> that doctrine that holds that the covenant of grace is not established upon conditions, and that nothing of performance is required on man's part to give him an interest in it, but only to believe that he is justified.[35]

In its most extreme form, antinomianism is indeed heretical to an orthodox Protestant. One use of the term indicates a sect specifically attacked by Luther himself,

> a sect which originated with John Agricola, a companion of Luther, about the year 1538. He is said to have held that as the church is not now under the law, but under the gospel, the ten commandments should not be taught to the people. Enemies said that he or his followers considered that a believer might sin at his pleasure [!], but this is believed to have been a calumny.[36]

---

[34] Ronald MacDonald, "George MacDonald: A Personal Note," in Frederick Watson, ed., *From a Northern Window*, James Nisbet & Co., London, 1911, p. 84.

[35] See *The Encyclopedic Dictionary*, Cassell & Co., London, 1909, article on "antinomianism."

[36] *Ibid.*

Calumny or not, the idea that a person could be saved without good works, or that he might redeem himself with one final act of repentance (in *Lilith* we see that this act might occur even after death) undercut the foundations of Protestant orthodoxy. While Marlowe's Faust is *not* allowed "one drop" as "Christ's blood streams in the firmament,"[37] MacDonald confidently writes that

> No man sinks into the grave, he only disappears. Life is a constant sunrise, which death cannot interrupt any more than the night can swallow up the sun.[38]

MacDonald, from a dogmatic perspective, might very well be seen as a heretic.

There is another perspective on salvation, however, a perspective that emphasizes the gospels.

> But Jesus said, Suffer little children, and forbid them not, to come unto me: for of such is the kingdom of heaven. (Matt. 19:14)

> Verily I say unto you, Whosoever shall not receive the kingdom of God as a little child, he shall not enter therein. (Mark 10:15)

To the Victorians, who saw children as the innocently wise, the notion that a person might regain childlike innocence, a notion approved by scripture, was a consoling thought indeed. MacDonald, even when writing for actual children, offers this consolation to the great mass of adults. In *At the Back of the North Wind*, the narrator is questioning the boy Diamond, the angelic hero of the tale. Diamond is always helping someone naively and well.

[37] Christopher Marlowe, *Doctor Faustus*, sc. xiv, ll.137-138.
[38] George MacDonald, *Helps For Weary Souls*, J. Dewey, ed., Thomas R. Knox & Co., New York, 1885, p. 41.

"What did the boy and girl want with you, Dia-
mond?" I asked.
"They had seen a creature [a shadow] that fright-
ened them."
"And they came to tell you about it?"
"They couldn't get water out of the well for it. So
they wanted me to go with them."
"They're both bigger than you."
"Yes, but they were frightened at it."
"And you weren't frightened at it?"
"No."
"Why?"
"Because I'm silly. I'm never frightened at things."
I could not help thinking of the old meaning of the
world *silly*.[39]

Although *silly* means frivolous now, it once indicated ap-
proximately the common ground between *blessed* and *innocent*. We see the same ambivalence in a word like *simple*,
which can mean either *pure*, and hence *powerful* ("a simple
truth"), or *mentally deficient*. By one perspective, simple,
silly, childlike innocence fulfills the gospels. To assert in
one's fiction, as MacDonald does, that a person can be re-
deemed through God's infinite Grace by a single acceptance
of humility might be viewed not as the antinomian heresy
but as a new substantiation of gospel truth.

In the age of Victoria, such a substantiation was of more
than passing interest.

If any real unity is to be ascribed to the Victorian era
in England, it must be found in two governing condi-
tions: first, there was no great war and no fear of catas-
trophe from without; and secondly, the whole period

---

[39] George MacDonald, *At the Back of the North Wind*, Airmont,
New York, 1966 (1871), p. 262.

was marked by interest in religious questions and was deeply influenced by seriousness of thought and self-discipline of character, an outcome of the Puritan ethos.[40]

MacDonald addressed this second concern directly. And on the same grounds that he tried to fulfill the gospels, his critics attacked him.

George McCrie wrote in 1875 of the "Aesthetics of Redemption." He felt that in reading *all* incidents in the Bible, "the sensation of admiration is produced; we involuntarily exclaim, 'How beautiful! this is the doing of the Lord.' "[41] A theologian like McCrie saw in writing the power of substantiation. In trying to create such beauty independently, rather than merely reporting the beauty of the Bible, MacDonald shows his "religious opinions . . . unsound and dangerous."[42] Like Father Brown, McCrie claims that illogic leads to bad theology:

> To reason with the heart instead of the head is always dangerous, but never more so than upon a subject like this [Redemption].[43]

> [MacDonald] trusts God so absolutely that he leaves his salvation to Him, utterly, fearlessly.[44]

The problem here, as with the question of too many or too few children, is that MacDonald's critics have a preconception of what is right and wrong. Their perspectives make fewer children better than more and make adherence to dogma superior to adherence to the spirit of the ministry of Jesus. This institutional reluctance becomes absolutely

---

[40] Trevelyan, *Illustrated Social History*, p. 107.
[41] George McCrie, *The Religion of Our Literature*, Hodder & Stoughton, London, 1875, p. 276.
[42] *Ibid.*, p. 295.    [43] *Ibid.*, p. 310.    [44] *Ibid.*, p. 305.

clear when Samuel Law Wilson complains that MacDonald simply makes Christianity *too easy* and so obviates the need for "all the moral appliances of evangelical religion."[45] And yet, perhaps because these theologians present the normative perspective of Victorian England, MacDonald's writings were and are popular, especially with the devout. For such people, *At the Back of the North Wind* (1871) and *Phantastes* (1858) offer an escape from the dogma of their religion, but do not require a slackening of faith. As Thomas Gunn Selby, another theologian contemporary to MacDonald, wrote:

> To know the chief characters of George MacDonald's . . . books is a means of grace, although we may demur to some of the things in the theology taught.[46]

The chief character of *At the Back of the North Wind* is a waif named Diamond who would gladden the mushy heart of Dickens. Diamond just plain doesn't understand bad language[47] and he automatically makes up songs that calm the savagery of alcohol[48] and quiet crying babies.[49] The central question of the book is that of theodicy, and MacDonald's answer is simple: the North Wind (whose other name is never mentioned but we know it is Death) is revealed as a perfect servant of some higher good (again unnamed, again we know: God) and therefore the narrative action (in which the North Wind, personified as a lady, becomes Diamond's best friend) justifies the doctrine of the fortunate fall. The Hyperborean region is gotten to by go-

[45] Samuel Law Wilson, D.D., *The Theology of Modern Literature*, T. T. Clark, Edinburgh, 1899, p. 287.

[46] Thomas Gunn Selby, *The Theology of Modern Fiction*, Charles H. Kelly, London, 1896, p. 132.

[47] MacDonald, *At the Back of the North Wind*, p. 129.

[48] *Ibid.*, p. 140.      [49] *Ibid.*, p. 121.

ing through death, and one dies into a better life of perfect communication, a fantastic reversal of human fears that echoes St. John of Patmos and predicts the later poetry of T. S. Eliot. As the narrator says in an interpolated original fairy tale called "Little Daylight," "I never knew of any interference on the part of a wicked fairy that did not turn out a good thing in the end."[50] MacDonald is fully aware of the conventions of his fantastic genre and uses them to escape the difficult theological problem of evil: he takes the bold step of calling death the best thing in the world. If man does not see it that way, he has the wrong perspective. As the narrator/hero of *Phantastes* says when he ends his tale:

> What we call evil, is the only and best shape, which, for the person and his condition at the time, could be assumed by the best good. And so, *Farewell.*[51]

The consolation of MacDonald came from fantastic reversals and was an escape both from a world of social turmoil and the rigors of a religion that did not help to make that turmoil bearable. " 'Surely,' " Diamond suggests, " 'it is good to be afflicted.' "[52]

One must make two points clear concerning MacDonald: first, he is a good writer; second, his theology has nearly won the day. MacDonald's style is characterized not only by a comforting, preaching kind of mysticism, but extraordinary description and ringing psychological insight. Diamond hears North Wind when she is of huge size, a storm personified, yet talking to her "silly" friend:

[50] *Ibid.*, p. 196.
[51] George MacDonald, *Phantastes*, in *Phantastes and Lilith*, C. S. Lewis, ed., Wm. B. Eerdmans, Grand Rapids, Mich., 1971 (1964), p. 182.
[52] MacDonald, *At the Back of the North Wind*, p. 192.

Her voice was like the bass of a deep organ, without
the groan in it; like the most delicate of violin tones
without the wail in it; like the most glorious of trumpet-
ejaculations without the defiance in it; like the sound
of falling water without the clatter and clash in it: it
was like all of them and neither of them—all of them
without their faults, each of them without its pecu-
liarity: after all, it was more like his mother's voice
than anything else in the world.[53]

This kind of parental, protective Christianity was nearly
heretical in the High Victorian generation; it had been actually heretical in the Renaissance; it is nearly orthodox today. C. S. Lewis, discussing mythmakers such as Novalis
and Kafka says, "MacDonald is the greatest genius of this
kind whom I know."[54] Indeed, in Lewis' allegorical *The
Great Divorce* (1946), when the I-narrator travels through
Heaven and Hell to learn how the universe is really consti-
tuted, instead of Vergil or Beatrice, he is guided by George
MacDonald. Protestant churches are today more forgiving
than they were a hundred years ago. And yet Lewis, like
many of the Victorians, fits his fantastic elements to his perspective on the audience. In his allegorical science fiction
trilogy for adults, the evil Dr. Weston dies and is damned;
in his Narnia chronicles for children, Aslan the Christ figure
often intervenes to encourage the spiritually saving return
to humility. When one can get away with it, as in addressing children, the gospel of forgiveness is not the antinomian
heresy.

MacDonald, however, had more theological strength than
Lewis. He seemed, in going from books for adults to books
for children, not to vary his underlying theology. *Phantastes*

[53] *Ibid.*, p. 54.
[54] C. S. Lewis, introduction to *Phantastes and Lilith*, p. 10.

offers the same kind of consolations against death that we find in *At the Back of the North Wind*. Again we find that these consolations depend upon fantastic reversals of our normal perspectives:

> . . . there is plenty of room for meeting
> in the universe. . . .[55]

> With a presence I am smitten
> Dumb, with a foreknown surprise.[56]

> The veil between, though very dark, is very thin.[57]

> Past tears are present strength.[58]

Like *At the Back of the North Wind*, *Phantastes* too has an interpolated fairy tale; *Phantastes* too has a main character (Anodos: he who finds the way up) whose powers are Orphic; *Phantastes* too takes consolation from the idea of dying into life. In the use of fairy tale, of the Orpheus myth, and of mystic rebirth, both these works are fantastic. The difference between the adult and the child literature does not reside in the uses of the fantastic. In the book intended for children, the main character is a boy who is innocent. His innocence is shown to be all powerful, and when at the end others think he is dead, the narrator says approvingly, "I knew that he had gone to the back of the north wind."[59] In the book for adults, the main character, following his twenty-first birthday, undergoes a series of humbling visions that take twenty-one days. In the course of these he dies and is reborn childlike, not to the back of the north wind but into his non-visionary life. *Phantastes* implies that a person may regain blessed innocence. From a theological perspective, the books are the same. Since the escape from

[55] MacDonald, *Phantastes*, p. 41.
[56] *Ibid.*, p. 118.   [57] *Ibid.*, p. 142.   [58] *Ibid.*, p. 149.
[59] MacDonald, *At the Back of the North Wind*, p. 288.

religion is offered most dramatically by the fantastic elements of the narrative, it is wholly fitting that the fantastic elements are not different in the two genres: MacDonald merely shows the adult and child version of the same thing. Notice the innocence/experience conjunction in MacDonald's own discussion of his works of imagination:

If any strain of my "broken music" makes a child's eyes flash, or his mother's grow dim, my labour will not have been in vain.[60]

Just as William Morris had offered an escape from history, both for children and for adults who would be as children, George MacDonald's Fantasies offered the Victorians an escape from their religion.

C. L. Dodgson was an Oxford teacher of mathematics. Like many other such men of his times, he was a non-preaching but nonetheless ordained clergyman. Like all other Oxbridge teachers who lived in house, he was unmarried. Unlike many others, however, but like both William Morris, who worked at everything, and George MacDonald, who wrote in at least four genres, C. L. Dodgson carried on a vast range of activities. His conformist activities, those that fulfilled the normative perspectives of the Victorian world, were either scientific or religious. His religious attainments were minor: he finally preached one sermon in the year of his death, and he wrote didactic and dull children's allegories like *Sylvie and Bruno* (1889 & 1893). In addition, he had many charities, especially those in aid of children.

His scientific accomplishments were of a different order. His textbook of Euclidean geometry was considered the

---

[60] George MacDonald, *A Dish of Orts*, Sampson Low Marston, London, 1893, p. 322.

finest of its day, and his work in symbolic logic, though it took a different tack from, and lost out to, Russell's, was a kind of high point in a particular line of the development of mathematical thinking.[61] Beyond these scholarly functions, Dodgson was a photographer, one of the two most influential English photographers of his century. Indeed, the best photographs we have of many of his contemporaries, including Tennyson and MacDonald, are by Dodgson.

But Dodgson escaped from his world of science, and he escaped from it under the name of Lewis Carroll. His use of the fantastic, because of his own logical perspective, is the most complete and rigorous rejection of logic in English. While Russell was developing non-syllogistic logics and the Germans and Russians were investigating non-Euclidean geometry, Dodgson was pursuing to their logical extremes the underlying principles of Newtonian commonsense science. He was in step with his era, pursuing the mathematics appropriate to a science that called Darwinian evolution "mechanistic" and that made history explainable in terms of "economic determinism."

Thomas S. Kuhn describes the way in which science normally proceeds under the guidance of intellectually controlling "paradigms."

> . . . the term 'paradigm' is used in two different senses. On the one hand, it stands for the entire constellation of beliefs, values, techniques, and so on shared by the members of a given community. On the other, it denotes one sort of element in that constellation, the concrete puzzle-solutions which, employed as models or

[61] See W. W. Bartley, III, "Lewis Carroll as Logician," in *TLS*, 15 June 1973, pp. 665-666.

examples, can replace explicit rules as a basis for the
solution of the remaining puzzles of normal science.[62]

In the High Victorian days of C. L. Dodgson, normal science held a mechanistic perspective that promised the inexorable solution of all problems if only they could be
stated in the proper terms. On this dependable basis, at the
end of this generation, H. G. Wells was able to initiate a
whole new genre of the "scientific romance." "Rules" served
to solve puzzles, and most of the situations of Victorian life
seemed to be mere puzzles as England and Englishmen
proceeded to fulfill their historically and religiously ordained destinies using every scientific tool at hand.

As a normative Victorian, in the same year that Wells
predicted social disaster in *The Time Machine* (1895),
C. L. Dodgson published *Pillow-Problems* (1895), a series
of mathematical puzzles. They were offered in the service
of a moralistic religion:

> Nor is it as a remedy for *wakefulness* that I have sug-
> gested mathematical calculation; but as a remedy for
> the *harassing thoughts* that are apt to invade a wholly-
> unoccupied mind.[63]

Lewis Carroll, however, published serially *A Tangled Tale*
(1880-1885), a loosely connected series of twelve logic
problems that made a children's story. Like other Victorians,
Dodgson/Carroll felt it easier to escape society's prescribed
perspectives when he could consider his audience to be
only innocent children.

The Alice books are rich in satire, parody, and lampoon;
they invert and reverse everything in sight. A consideration

---

[62] Thomas S. Kuhn, *The Structure of Scientific Revolutions*, University of Chicago Press, Chicago, 1970 (1962), p. 175.

[63] Charles L. Dodgson, *Pillow-Problems* (1895), in Lewis Carroll,
*Pillow Problems and A Tangled Tale*, Dover, New York, 1958, p. x.

of the structure of *Through the Looking Glass* may make clearer the fact that the Alice books are in all ways fantastic because, at bottom, their Fantasy is the escape from logic. The Looking Glass world is in every regard a reversal of the normative world. An exhaustive demonstration of this takes most of the glosses in the second half of Martin Gardner's voluminous and excellent *The Annotated Alice*. However, we might well recall that, like any other normal puzzle, *Through the Looking Glass* begins with a statement of its beginning configuration and its rules. Its rules are those of chess, and its configuration is the relation of the characters (pieces) as they are initially placed in Looking Glass land, a land whose columns are neatly divided by very English hedges and whose ranks are divided by convenient little brooks. Carroll proceeds to tell the story and the pieces advance. However, each time Alice crosses a brook, despite the comforting presence, indeed dominance, of the "rules," she fantastically arrives in a totally different landscape. Checkerboards are nothing if not regular; Looking Glass land is nothing if not an assault on that regularity. The assault is the more complete because the rules are presumed to operate.

Many of Humpty Dumpty's remarks serve as miniature examples of this process whereby Carroll uses the mechanistic perspectives of his contemporary science to fantastically escape the world in which those perspectives are valid.

> ". . . but tell me your name and your business."
>
> "My *name* is Alice, but—"
>
> "It's a stupid name enough!" Humpty Dumpty interrupted impatiently. "What does it mean?"
>
> "*Must* a name mean something?" Alice asked doubtfully.

"Of course it must," Humpty Dumpty said with a short laugh: "*my* name means the shape I am—and a good handsome shape it is, too. With a name like yours, you might be any shape, almost."[64]

In logic, as in grammar, there are two kinds of names: common and proper. A common name *must* indeed have a universal meaning, *person, statue, book*; a proper name usually has no such meaning but rather signifies a particular thing, *Alice, the Statue of Liberty, Through the Looking Glass.* Humpty Dumpty says that this latter phenomenon should be reversed. (Soon after he claims that words mean whatever he wants them to, and thereby reverses his position as well.)[65] This apparent reversal of the rules of logic is itself apparently reversed, however. On the basis of these new rules, Humpty Dumpty says that Alice "might be any shape." But that, of course, cannot be, because regardless of the *names* of things, and whether or not those *names* have particular or universal meanings, the shapes of the things remain the same. Carroll asks us to look out for this failure of the reversal to reverse by making Humpty Dumpty say, "almost." And yet, in Wonderland (though not in Looking Glass land), Alice *was* "any shape, almost," and Humpty Dumpty's reversal of normal logic is seen to work whether the name reversal obtains or not. Because the fantastic reversals involved in this dialogue are really reversals at the level of the underlying logic of both Alice's worlds and ours, this Fantasy offers an escape from those very perspectives on which normal Victorian science was based. Perhaps the continuing power of mechanistic science to dominate our own perspectives, even in a post-quantum

---

[64] Lewis Carroll, *Through the Looking Glass*, in *The Annotated Alice*, Martin Gardner, ed., World Publishing Company, New York, 1960, p. 263.
[65] *Ibid.*, p. 269.

physics world, explains in part why Carroll's works today are more popular than those of Dodgson, MacDonald, or Morris.

Note that each of these writers offered an escape precisely from the perspective that dominated his non-fantasizing activities, the energetic Morris seeking an "epoch of rest," the sermonizing MacDonald standing theology on its head, the scientific Carroll reversing the fundamental tenets of his science. This common use of the fantastic is not the only connection among these men: as diverse as they were in habit, temperament, areas of activity, and social station, they were nonetheless related to each other in the real world of Victorian London. Morris lived from 1878 until his death in 1896 in a house in Upper Hammersmith Mall he called Kelmscott House. From 1867 until 1877, this same house had been called the Retreat, and had been occupied by the family of George MacDonald.[66] It was the advice of Mary and Greville, two of the MacDonald children, that initially induced Lewis Carroll to publish *Alice's Adventures in Wonderland*.[67] Sir John Tenniel, *Punch* cartoon editor for half a century and the illustrator of *Alice*, took great pleasure in parodying in his drawings the work of the Pre-Raphaelites. Morris was one of these; and so was Arthur Hughes, the life-long friend of George MacDonald and illustrator of almost every one of his books. Victorian England in this generation from 1860 to 1895 was in many regards a tightly knit generation, a generation of stability.

[66] The only biography of George MacDonald is the somewhat cosmetic *George MacDonald and His Wife*, Dial Press, New York, 1924, written by one of George's sons, Greville MacDonald, himself a friend of Carroll, a respected physician, and an author of forgettable children's books.

[67] This delightful coincidence is reported in another fascinating and cosmetic biography, *The Life and Letters of Lewis Carroll*, Century, New York, 1896, written by Stuart Dodgson Collingwood, a nephew.

In addition to their respective major aims, Morris poked at religion and science in his works, MacDonald at history and science, and Carroll at history and to some extent religion. Yet in finding a "perspective" that tends to "unify" the work of each of these men, we are able to use the particular analysis of what makes a work fantastic to supplement and refine the usual kinds of socio-literary study of worldview. Seeing that these men are related by history as well as by generic choice, we can predict that some of the fantastic literature of the High Victorian period would have a somewhat more thorough mixture of escapes from these three perspectives: *history* as inexorable linear progress toward English self-fulfillment, *religion* as a call to a duty above forgiveness, and *science* as a mechanistic solution to any imaginable puzzle. In *Erewhon* (1872), Samuel Butler offers us a work that mixes all these escapes.

The title of *Erewhon* is an anagram, nearly a mirror reversal of *Nowhere*. As such it calls to mind Looking Glass land or More's *Utopia* (no-place), and suggests that its contents will be a denial of some other land. That other land, of course, is Butler's contemporary Victorian England. The subtitle of this scattershot satire is *Over the Range*, and our adventuring narrator, we soon discover, has embarked on yet another Victorian reversal of the Hyperborea myth. The land he finds is a reversal of everything stable in Victorian England, and by the case Butler makes for the alternatives, the real-world norms look bad indeed. Science is criticized in ways large and small. The famous "Book of the Machines" turns Darwinism on its head and postulates that machines are evolving (why, just look at how much more efficient they are getting and how much more men are slaves to them) while this evolution is accomplished using man himself as the tool of propagation. More fundamentally, Newtonian commonsense science is hit with quick insights such as this:

> It is only the very great and good who have any living faith in the simplest axioms; and there are few who are so holy as to feel that 19 and 13 make 32 as certainly as 2 and 2 make 4.[68]

Religion too is attacked in the person of the "straighteners" who are crypto-clerics and base their ministrations to human misfortune not on the actions of people but on the application of pre-existing categories to those people. In detail, we find again such quips as this aimed at deflating the orthodox view of original sin:

> "To be born," they say, "is a felony—it is a capital crime, for which sentence may be executed at any moment after the commission of the offence."[69]

This parallels Woody Allen's assertion that "death is an acquired trait,"[70] and like that comment achieves its force because one can recognize in it the very perspective it denies. Just as Allen's remark uses modern evolutionary genetics to cast doubt on the superiority, say, of man over endlessly sub-dividing amoebae, so Butler's remark uses the guilt rhetoric of Victorian orthodoxy to cast doubt on the charity that is presumed to underlie Evangelical religion.

This reversal is at the heart of *Erewhon*. The land over the range is a comparatively pastoral land (and therefore on the face of it a likely candidate for utopia) because centuries before our narrator arrived the people destroyed most machines. Machine evolution, and machine competi-

---

[68] Samuel Butler, *Erewhon*, E. P. Dutton, 1910 (1872), p. 203.
[69] *Ibid.*, p. 145.
[70] Woody Allen, *Getting Even*, Warner, New York, 1972, p. 85.

tion, scared the Erewhonians. To avoid displacement, they stopped history. In similar ways, this topsy-turvy thinking informs every social norm of Erewhon. Criminals, for instance, are put in hospitals while the sick are imprisoned. Each item in the catalog of Butler's ironic twists touches the underlying fabric of Victorianism. This book is sometimes criticized as too diverse, a breach of the decorum of organic form. Yet it was enormously popular and well thought of in its own time, and its popularity has endured. We might well suggest that the superficial chaos of *Erewhon* merely overlays a deeper form constructed of satiric and fantastic reversal. That the perspectives reversed are themselves conflated in the coherent and recognizable worldview of the High Victorian generation may well account for the felt coherence of the attacks of Butler's text. *Erewhon* is not merely an unusually popular fantastic journey; it answers to the needs of a generation. This becomes clear when the perspectives of that generation are made clear. Such clarity emerges not from the study of the normal alone, but from the complementary study of the normal and the fantastic.

# ❦IV❧
# The Fantastic and Genre Criticism

GENRE criticism is criticism of works of art distributed into classes. In the study of art, *genre* means *class*. In literature, classes are defined in diverse ways, many inconsistent with each other. For example, one might wish to study the genre of Elizabethan tragedies; that is, works written in English, during the reign of Elizabeth I, intended for stage performance, and having something to do with the fall of great personages. Elizabeth died in 1603; *King Lear* was written in 1606. But still *King Lear* is Elizabethan, if not in date, then in mood, and surely a matter of three years shouldn't prevent a work from being considered in its proper context. Propriety here reflects the perspectives of the reader, of the observer for whom selecting works along certain lines seems interesting and profitable. One could as well define a genre only by the number of verse lines, like the sonnet; or define a genre by its political content, like Marxist literature. The choice of a genre definition, a choice habitually made both conventionally and unconsciously, is a choice that reflects the perspectives of the reader. When we recommend one book to a friend as being "like" another, the grounds for similarity can be almost anything, so long as they include those elements of the work that we believe have made the first book valuable to our friend. Such a recommendation is an act of genre criticism.

The wide range of works which we have already seen fit to call, in one degree or another, fantastic, is large, much too large to constitute a single genre. We have embraced

117

whole conventional genres, such as fairy tale, detective story, and Fantasy,[1] and we have seen that as genres they may be related according to the degree and kind of their use of the fantastic. For this very reason, study of those elements that make a work fantastic gives us a new vantage on works previously classed only according to established generic divisions. The previous chapter explored methods by which consideration of the fantastic can yield information and analyses that complement the normal study of worldview. This chapter will explore methods by which consideration of the fantastic can yield information and analyses that complement the normal study of genres.

The term *science fiction* has been forced into many dif-

---

[1] The only theoretical work specifically on Fantasy is Tzvetan Todorov, *The Fantastic: A Structural Approach to a Literary Genre*, Richard Howard, transl., Case Western Reserve University Press, 1973 (1970). This is a book with many excellences which, in numerous ways, complements the current study. However, in many regards, these two works are in serious disagreement. An exhaustive comparison would needlessly sidetrack this inquiry, but two points may be worth making. First, Todorov radically limits not only Fantasy, but the fantastic, to the realm of a single genre. "Not all fictions . . . are linked to the fantastic" (p. 75), he writes, even though he recognizes that the fantastic is generated by "as if," which I would see, with Worringer, as inherent in all art. Second, Todorov locates the affect of the fantastic in "the reader's hesitation" (p. 32) in determining whether a narrated event must be taken as merely metaphoric (moving the text into a genre he calls the *marvelous*) or actual (moving the text into a genre he calls the *uncanny*). "The fantastic occupies the duration of this uncertainty" (p. 25). This is an acute and useful insight; however, it must be modified in two ways to capitalize on it. First, this hesitation should be seen not in relation to external norms, but rather in relation to microcontextual variations; second, one must realize that keeping track of this affect, and locating it in aspects of narrative other than plot, can give us an organizing principle for studies larger than those of Todorov's "literary genre." His is a thoughtful, suggestive, and useful book— one that anticipates some of the work here—but it is a book that ultimately reflects a different view of the fantastic.

ferent kinds of service.[2] Although coined by Hugo Gerns-
back in 1926 to denote the all-male technological adventure
stories he was writing and editing, the term has since been
made to include the voyage to Laputa in *Gulliver's Travels*
(1726) and the *Icaromenippus* of Lucian of Samosota
(b. 120 A.D.); it includes "Sword and Sorcery" novels like
*A Private Cosmos*, by Philip José Farmer, and rigorously
logical tales like the robotics stories of Isaac Asimov; it includes the sweetly lyrical romanticism of Ray Bradbury in
*The Martian Chronicles* and the unashamed machismo mili-
tarism of Robert A. Heinlein in *Starship Troopers*; it includes novels of warning and prediction like Nevil Shute's
*On the Beach* and such historic impossibilities as novels of
alternate time-streams like Moorcock's *The Warlord of the
Air*; it includes such enthusiastically technological tales as
the "Star Trek" series begun by James Blish and such
a-technological tales as *A Canticle for Leibowitz*, Walter M.
Miller, Jr.'s exploration of institutional stability and historical periodicity. And there are other works by these and
other authors that slip in and out of the genre with hardly
anyone's noticing.

One definition that seems to encompass the diverse works
we have mentioned is this: a work belongs in the genre of
science fiction if its narrative world is at least somewhat different from our own, and if that difference is apparent
against the background of an organized body of knowledge.
Some qualifications may make this definition clearer.

---

[2] See Robert Scholes and Eric S. Rabkin, *Science Fiction: History,
Science, Vision*, Oxford University Press, New York, 1977. A readable
layman's introduction to the genre is Sam J. Lundwall, *Science Fiction: What It's All About*, Ace Books, New York, 1971. A thorough
review of the field, concentrating on the novel from 1800 to the
present, is Brian W. Aldiss, *Billion Year Spree*, Schocken, New York,
1973. This book by a science fiction author is sufficiently capacious
to be forgiven its subtitle: "The True History of Science Fiction."

As with the fantastic, the notion of difference, though generally definable in relation to "our" world, actually must be defined in terms of the world outside the text as that text recreates it. Although today we have speedy and deadly submarines, *20,000 Leagues Under the Sea* (1869) is still science fiction for two reasons: first, Professor Aronnax makes clear that the science of Verne's day would never expect ships to be sunk by submarine ("the theory of an underwater *Monitor* was definitively rejected"),[3] and second, the grapholect of the text recalls the pre-submarine era. Difference then, in defining science fiction, refers to a microcontextual variation. When this variation is a full 180° reversal of a ground rule (for example, in a quantum mechanics dominated tale, the action might suddenly depend on the anti-expected phenomenon of speeds faster than that of light) then the science fiction tale is fantastic. If the variation is merely a use of the dis-expected (for example, intelligent life that reproduces by fission), then the tale is much less fantastic. The variation from accepted knowledge is one of the defining characteristics of the genre of science fiction, and it is a characteristic that we can use to subdivide carefully the genre for purposes of analysis.

A second qualification to our definition concerns the notion of an organized body of knowledge. The term *science*

---

[3] Jules Verne, *20,000 Leagues Under the Sea*, Anthony Bonner, transl., Bantam, New York, 1962 (1869), p. 20. Interestingly enough, Aronnax's lengthy protestations were as necessary for the 1869 audience as they are for us in establishing the science fiction reversal of the novel, for the first functional submarine (*The Turtle*) took part in the American Revolution, and in 1807 Robert Fulton, to Verne's own knowledge, demonstrated a working submarine in the Seine. Verne's reputation as a predictor of technological innovation rests not so much on his prescience as on his ability to create a narrative reality for which he predicts what he knows already to have been developed in the world outside his texts. The fantastic depends on reversal of the ground rules of the *narrative* world.

calls hardware to mind, but much science fiction really makes only subordinate use of technology. The real "science" behind Ursula K. Leguin's study of the social importance of sex as a role indicator (*The Left Hand of Darkness*, 1969) is anthropology, not physics or chemistry or even biology. In *Pavane* (1966), by Keith Roberts, we have a world set in the mid-1960s, but it concerns the history of a world that shared our history until 1588, at which point the Spanish fleet *conquered* the English. The consistency of Roberts' alternative world depends on extrapolations of the laws of history, economic determinism, scientific evolution. What is important in the definition of science fiction is not the appurtenances of ray guns and lab coats, but the "scientific" habits of mind: the idea that paradigms do control our view of all phenomena, that within these paradigms all normal problems can be solved, and that abnormal occurrences must either be explained or initiate the search for a better (usually more inclusive) paradigm. In science fiction, these habits of mind and their associated bodies of knowledge determine the outcome of events, regardless of which science most obviously informs the narrative world. In that regard, like the puzzle tales of detective fiction, all science fiction is to some extent fantastic.

A special case of this definition by difference and organized body of knowledge is this prescription: a good work of science fiction makes one and only one assumption about its narrative world that violates our knowledge about our own world and then extrapolates the whole narrative world from that difference. In letting the Spanish armada *win*, *Pavane* satisfies this reduced definition (though many other works, like *A Voyage to Arcturus*, do not). This truncated prescription has great heuristic power. Modern science fiction developed most strongly in the United States, and then England. For both these communities, the primary antecedent was H. G. Wells, and Wells followed this prescription instinctively. In *The Time Machine* (1895), for example, we are told in italics:

> *There is no difference between Time and any of the three dimensions of Space except that our consciousness moves along it.*[4]

Granted this fantastic assumption, Wells proceeds to journey to his famous future in which industrialism has made the leisure class into effete and useless children (Eloi) and the working class into loveless and ruthless monsters (Morlocks). Wells had studied (1884-1887) with evolutionist T. H. Huxley, and was to be one of the most distinguished members (1903-1908) of the socialist Fabian Society. *The Time Machine* uses the fantastic idea of time travel (a reversal of the perspectives of classical mechanics) to present a vivid social warning based on orthodox extrapolations of the biology and political science current at the end of the century.

Understanding that the field is broader than the prescriptive definition we can use to locate the works of Wells, we can still take *The Time Machine* as a paradigmatic work of science fiction. Another work that satisfies even the Wellsian purist definition of science fiction is Theodore Sturgeon's *More Than Human* (1953), a novel of the emergence of man's superior future. A comparison of this work with Arthur C. Clarke's *Childhood's End* (1953) will show one of the ways by which consideration of the fantastic can complement normal genre criticism.

*More Than Human* is a very well-written work. In the year following its publication, it was awarded the International Fantasy Award by a panel of critics selected at the

[4] H. G. Wells, *The Time Machine*, Berkley Highland, New York, 1963 (1895), p. 7.

British (science fiction) convention. In this novel, we read of the emergence of "*Homo Gestalt*, the next step upward . . . why not a psychic evolution instead of the physical?"[5] This is the assumption we need to grant. The Gestalt creature we are primarily concerned with is a coordinated telepathic entity made up of two teleports (Beanie and Bonnie, the apparently idiotic twin offspring of a janitor), a telekine (Janie, who can make objects move through space, or non-space, at will), a computational super-brain (Baby, a non-verbal, non-growing grotesque change-of-life baby, who communicates by direct telepathy with Janie and through her with the non-senders Beanie and Bonnie), and a Head. The story proceeds as pure science fiction if we grant that people, especially emotional people, and especially children, have potential psychic powers if only these are not obscured by education; that is, if these powers are not repressed by social training and its primary tool, verbal communication.

The book opens with Lone, an adult idiot who is sensitive to the telepathic signals of children because he is a wild creature himself, having escaped an orphanage and somehow learned to survive in the woods. Introduced next is Janie, a child whose enormous hate keeps her telekinetic powers useable (for instance, she "thinks" an ashtray at one of her mother's lovers and floors him).[6] By great good chance, Beanie and Bonnie's father is the janitor in the building in which Janie lives. The teleports and the telekine communicate telepathically, become friends, and run away together.

By great good luck again, these wandering children somehow appeal emotionally to Lone's idiotic telepathic re-

[5] Theodore Sturgeon, *More Than Human*, Farrar, Straus and Young, New York, 1953, p. 220.
[6] *Ibid.*, p. 32.

ceptors. He takes them in and they begin to function together. Later Lone takes in the freakish and abandoned Baby, who becomes the brain of *Homo Gestalt*. Janie, the only full telepath and therefore the communication center of the group, plugs Baby into the non-verbal network and she reports that "Baby was matching every fact she fed him with every other fact that he had been fed previously."[7] *Homo Gestalt* begins to function.

The vocabulary of *teleports* and *telekines*, the computational abilities of Baby, and the careful reporting of the coincidences that slowly went into the accumulation of *Homo Gestalt* imply the perspectives of normal mid-twentieth-century science. However, one question nags at the reader: what is the value of an apparently scientific explanation if the odds against any one of these occurrences (the mere existence of teleports, for example) seem astronomical; how much less scientific the explanation seems when one considers the multiplied odds against Janie's living in the right apartment building, meeting Lone, and so on. This question of coincidence seems to undercut the novel as an example of pure Wellsian science fiction.

In the second part of the novel, we concentrate on Gerry Thompson, a hating young man who finally comes to be the new, and much improved, Head when Lone dies. Gerry alone can kill a man or absorb his memory by mere eye contact; he can force someone to do his will. With Gerry as Head, *Homo Gestalt* has multiplied power, and Gerry's will is now informed by the capabilities of the group entity. *Homo Gestalt* is a potentially terrible beast, but a terrible beast with nothing much to do. Money is easy, and then what? Janie refuses to cooperate when Gerry decides to exercise their collective power for evil, and together they have no corporate vision for good.

[7] *Ibid.*, p. 71.

In the last part of the book, Janie on her own rehabilitates Hip Barrows, whose mind had been nearly destroyed years earlier by Gerry. Hip is, once reconstructed, very bright, but not psychic in any way. Still, he is convinced that he must revenge himself against Gerry. However, when the showdown comes, and Hip has a knife at Gerry's throat, he drops the knife in order to give Gerry a moral education. The shock of kindness is so strong that Gerry pauses to read Hip's mind and motives. Gerry thus learns shame and the scales fall from his eyes. Hip, the non-psychic, is suddenly revealed as a necessary part of *Homo Gestalt*, "the still small voice"[8] without which the new being cannot properly exist. With Hip plugged in through Janie, and Gerry chastened by Hip, *Homo Gestalt* can begin to function. It's an appealing idea, appealing especially because Sturgeon has created it in such a way that someone like the reader, rather than a telepath, is the keystone of this glorious evolution. A place is made for us. But then, this place can exist only if the other improbable five exist and, against fantastic odds, find each other. The unlikelihood of this seems to make the book illogical; seems to make the book fail as an escape; and seems to prevent the book from actually fulfilling the requirements of its genre.

As soon as Hip has become integrated into *Homo Gestalt*, however, the narrative changes tone as new awarenesses flood upon Gerry and the other members of his Gestalt:

> For a long time the only sound was Gerry's difficult breathing. Suddenly even this stopped, as something happened, something—spoke.
> It came again.
> *Welcome.*
> The voice was a silent one. And here, another, silent

[8] *Ibid.*, p. 231.

too, but another for all that. *It's a new one. Welcome, child!*

Still another: *Well, well, well! We thought you'd never make it.* . . .

Gerry clapped his hands to his mouth. His eyes bulged. Through his mind came a hush of welcoming music. There was warmth and laughter and wisdom.[9]

Gerry's Gestalt has been accepted by the community of Gestalts. We suddenly realize that the coincidences had not been far-fetched at all. The assertion that there are other *Homo Gestalts* implies that telepaths do exist, but we just don't know about them. Our knowledge has been limited by Gerry's, and his had been limited by the other Gestalts. Gerry's Gestalt had thought that it was alone in the world, but only because the other *Homo Gestalts* who had come together earlier for the good of humanity had "quarantined" it.[10] Once made complete by the addition of "the still small voice," Gerry's Gestalt can learn, and we can too, that such Gestalts have been forming, indeed, *guiding* the formation of other Gestalts, all along. By a single stroke, Sturgeon explains logically the one remaining doubt that mars the organic integrity of the book as a work of science fiction. With causation explained precisely on the grounds that we have accepted all along as the *single* allowable deviation from known phenomena, the book achieves unity. This emergent unity seems to justify the immediately following notion that in these *Homo Gestalts* "at last was power which could not corrupt."[11] Since the parts are replaceable, the entity is immortal,[12] and therefore *Homo Gestalt* is, in fact, angelic. Man, with us included as the Hip Barrowses of the world, is shown a vision of heaven. The last line of the book refers to Gerry no longer the vengeful telepath but Gerry

[9] *Ibid.*          [10] *Ibid.*, p. 232.          [11] *Ibid.*, p. 233.
[12] *Ibid.*, p. 224.

the *Homo Gestalt*: "And humbly, he joined their company."[13]

*Childhood's End*, published in the same year as *More Than Human*, has a great deal in common with it. Although it won no award in its time, readers of Clarke will assert that his book is as well written as Sturgeon's. In fact, *Childhood's End* has become perhaps the most popular single book of science fiction today. It certainly outranks *More Than Human*.[14] Like that book, *Childhood's End* concerns the emergence of the next step in man's evolution, a step taken by children into a new species of telepathic communion and overwhelming telekinetic power. Clarke is perhaps even more insistent than Sturgeon on the importance, less the telepathy assumption, of the rule of normal science. Man is held in thrall by an advanced and astonishingly long-lived race called the "Overlords." Their technological power is awesome and, through Rikki Stormgren, the Secretary General of the United Nations, they rule earth utterly. Stormgren speaks with one Overlord only, Karellen.

"You know why Wainwright [a religious leader] and his kind fear me, don't you?" asked Karellen. His voice was somber now, like a great organ rolling its notes from a high cathedral nave. "You will find men like him in all the world's religions. They know that we represent reason and science, and, however confident they may be in their beliefs, they fear that we will overthrow their gods. Not necessarily through any deliberate act, but in a subtler fashion. Science can destroy religion by ignoring it as well as by disproving its tenets. No one ever demonstrated, so far as I am aware, the nonexistence of Zeus or Thor, but they have few

13 *Ibid.*, p. 233.
14 Jack Williamson, *Science Fiction Comes To College*, privately printed, 1971, p. 14.

followers now. The Wainwrights fear, too, that we know the truth about the origins of their faiths. How long, they wonder, have we been observing humanity? Have we watched Mohammed begin the hegira, or Moses giving the Jews their laws? Do we know all that is false in the stories they believe?"[15]

Science is clearly central to this novel. The basis of the story is modern Darwinian evolution. The Overlords are nursemaids for the human race. Given current trends, Overlord science predicts, man will soon irradiate himself. Man, however, is potentially *Homo Gestalt* (though Clarke doesn't use this term), and for the sake of that newer man, Karellen and company control the life of current man. Like children, we are to be protected against ourselves. When Total Breakthrough[16] occurs, when man's children all at once and everywhere on the planet, mutate into *Homo Gestalt*, we have childhood's end.

The relation between the Overlords and *Homo sapiens* is explained at length in terms of Darwinian evolution.

". . . there are many races in the universe, and some of them discovered these [telepathic] powers long before your species—or mine—appeared on the scene. They have been waiting for you to join them, and now the time has come. . . . probably, like most men, you have always regarded us as your masters. That is not true. We have never been more than guardians, doing a duty imposed upon us from—above. . . . we are the midwives. But we ourselves are barren."[17]

[15] Arthur C. Clarke, *Childhood's End*, Ballantine, New York, 1972 (1953), p. 23.
[16] *Ibid.*, p. 175.
[17] *Ibid.*, p. 176.

". . . we represent the ends of two different evolutions. . . . Our potentialities are exhausted, but yours are still untapped."[18]

The Overlords, not only to serve the "Overmind,"[19] but, in order to learn how they themselves might make Total Breakthrough, have restrained and guided man for a hundred years. They have interdicted man's progress with the old anti-science fears of the nineteenth century ("The stars are not for man")[20] only to have man grow, under the rule of evolution, into a mind-thing that can inhabit the stars, or the voids between them, with perfect ease. Like Hip's role in *More Than Human*, the "epidemic"[21] that affects all human children, but which can never affect the Overlords, shows ordinary man superior to his apparent master.

Unlike Sturgeon, Clarke reverses the science on which his book relies. Every student of evolution knows that, although one species is thought to emerge by discontinuous mutation from the loins of a previous species, this is seen *always* as occurring in one individual at a time. If the trait is successful, then it spreads and eventually a new species emerges. Clarke throws all that to the winds and, despite talk about evolutionary lines, postulates the whole human race moving on into a new and perfectly communal era. Where the nagging doubt is scientized in Sturgeon, science is spiritualized in Clarke. From the standpoint of aesthetic unity within the decorum of the genre of Wellsian science fiction, Clarke's book is clearly inferior to Sturgeon's; from the standpoint of popularity, however, Sturgeon's book is just as clearly inferior to Clarke's. This relation between the two books can be explained by considering how each uses the fantastic.

[18] *Ibid.*, pp. 182-83.  [19] *Ibid.*  [20] *Ibid.*, p. 137.
[21] *Ibid.*, p. 179.

Sturgeon uses the fantastic in the paradigmatic way pre-scribed for Wellsian science fiction. The world becomes ordered (as it does in fairy tales and detective fiction), that order taking its specific rules from the body of normal sci-ence known at the time of writing. Clarke, though still fall-ing well within our general definition for science fiction, falls outside Wellsian science fiction by virtue of his rejec-tion of the narratively operative assumption of modern evo-lution. This rejection, this sudden reversal of a ground rule of its narrative world, is a central episode in *Childhood's End*. This episode is paradigmatically fantastic. The aston-ishment of the adults at their mutated children provides signals enough. Somehow, this novel, which is too fantastic to be pure science fiction, is a work of science fiction more popular than its better done, award-winning parallel.

The particular fantasy that Clarke indulges is the Chris-tian fantasy of the descent of Grace. The coming of Total Breakthrough, like the Second Coming, represents salvation for all men not already corrupt. Sturgeon and Clarke agree that children are innocent and adults corrupt. However, Sturgeon sees ordinary man achieving salvation through individual acts of bravery (as when Hip releases the lethal Gerry), while Clarke sees all men achieving salvation through divine intercession. Sturgeon's salvation is a creed for this world; Clarke's salvation is eschatological. *Child-hood's End* is an aptly chosen title.

The notion of the Second Coming, the idea that God may intervene and save us all, gives rise to the antinomian heresy that we saw in C. S. Lewis' children's literature and that runs throughout the Fantasies of George MacDonald. North Wind tells Diamond that " 'I'm either not a dream, or there's something better that's not a dream.' "[22] When a

[22] George MacDonald, *At the Back of the North Wind*, Airmont, New York, 1966 (1871), p. 275.

father in *Childhood's End* is told about the dreams of one of his mutating children (mutating not at conception but after formation, thus again violating normal science), he remarks that

> "I never believed that they were simply the imaginings of a child. They were so incredible that—I know this sounds ridiculous—they *had* to be based on some reality."[23]

This is a faith in the "Aesthetics of Redemption." When Total Breakthrough occurs, the children of Man float off into space. They are, in terms of literary structural parallels, on their way to heaven.

Clarke's work, then, shares something of the theology of the Fantasist MacDonald, although its readiest generic label and its most visible structural features align it with Sturgeon. When we recognize the religious understructure of *Childhood's End*, we change the emphasis we put on individual incidents. For example, when read as a story of quasi-scientific, utopian science fiction, the incidents centering on Stormgren seem to be merely embellishments, games played with characterization to humanize the tale. However, viewed as a rewrite of the Bible, this judgment changes. When Stormgren is near death, he visits Karellen for the last time. They have always spoken through a one-way window and no man has ever (to that point) looked upon an Overlord. Stormgren, the faithful servant, asks that he be allowed this. At the end of the interview, for the first time, a light comes on on Karellen's side of the window: a chair, twice the size of a man, and, just going through a closing door, the back of a being! Stormgren is grateful for this privileged glimpse, muses on Karellen's guardianship, and hopes that in the future when Karellen can come to

[23] Clarke, *Childhood's End*, p. 173.

earth he will "stand beside the grave of the first man ever to be his friend."[24] In Exodus, God and Moses argue frequently about the best way to educate those foolish people who will persist in making golden calves. Moses says,

> I beseech thee, shew me thy glory. . . .
> And he said, Thou canst not see my face: for there shall no man see me, and live.
> And the Lord said, Behold, *there* is a place by me, and thou shalt stand upon a rock:
> And it shall come to pass, while my glory passeth by, that I will put thee in a clift of the rock, and will cover thee with my hand while I pass by:
> And I will take away mine hand, and thou shalt see my back parts: but my face shall not be seen.
> (Exodus 33:18-23)

Judged by the standards of Wellsian science fiction, *More Than Human* is a better book than *Childhood's End*. This is so precisely because Clarke's novel is in a significant regard the more fantastic. Once the narrative ground rules are created, the fantastic is proscribed from Wellsian science fiction. However, Clarke's book is by far the more popular. It would seem that either we throw out the notion of the aesthetic importance of organic unity or else we recognize that our genre label of *science fiction* has led us astray. This latter conclusion, of course, is the correct one. Within the decorum of the more fantastic *Childhood's End*, Clarke creates an organic unity every bit as complete as Sturgeon's. One should recall that Karellen's voice is initially described as "like a great organ rolling its notes from a high cathedral nave." Clarke has, by participation in the structures and images of Christianity, prepared us well for the Second Coming, for Total Breakthrough. When it comes, this fan-

[24] *Ibid.*, pp. 64-65.

tastic event may contradict normal science, but it is easily accommodated by a reader trained in the underlying image-structure of the book. Perhaps because the hope that Christianity—and Clarke—holds out is such a wholesale hope, the flawed science fiction is perceived as the better fiction.

This comparison indicates that genre labels, even when carefully attached to definitions, may play us false. In this example, it was important to know not only that these works were science fictions but that one was more fantastic than the other. Further, by comparing the use of the fantastic not to another work in the genre but to another work (Exodus) that makes the same use of the fantastic, we can better understand how Clarke's book functions, better see its hidden artistry, and better understand its effects on a large readership.

One can imagine a *continuum of the fantastic* that arranges all works within the genre of science fiction according to their degree of use of the fantastic. At one end of the scale we would find *I, Robot*, at the other *A Voyage to Arcturus*. This exercise in arrangement is hardly frivolous. Just as the application of genre distinctions has often led readers to new insights about literature, so application of continuum distinctions may also, as in the Sturgeon/Clarke comparison, yield new insights also, insights that directly complement those of normal genre criticism.

Isaac Asimov's *I, Robot* is a collection of stories loosely bound together by the character of Susan Calvin, a world renowned "robopsychologist," and by the Laws of Robotics that govern the robots of the stories. One might wish to read the volume as a composite novel. Whether read separately or together, though, each story constructs its ground rules on two premises: normal science operates, and positronic brains exist.

A positronic brain presumably is an artificial, programmable brain that is nonetheless equivalent to a human brain in responsiveness, infinitely more adept at numerical manipulation, and small enough to fit into a head-sized projection atop a man-shaped and man-sized metal body. By "law," and by ground rules, each positronic brain has irrevocably programmed into it the "Three Laws of Robotics":

1-A robot may not injure a human being, or, through inaction, allow a human being to come to harm.

2-A robot must obey the orders given it by human beings except where such orders would conflict with the First Law.

3-A robot must protect its own existence as long as such protection does not conflict with the First or Second Law.[25]

One can see how such a hierarchy of laws makes possible the creation of highly interesting logic games. In "Runaround," for example, a robot is told to "Go lose yourself." It chooses to join a shipment of identical robots. Now, how to retrieve the robot? The command was only "an expression" to a human, but literal law to the robot. A look at the table of laws will show that the only way to get a robot to break a command is by invoking the First Law. The problem then becomes to get the robot to reveal itself in order to prevent a human being from coming to harm. The catch is that the robot must perceive the human to be in immediate danger. If the robot, a highly intelligent creation, knows that the human will be saved at the last instant, then it will take no action at all, no matter how critical the situation might appear to a human.

This problem, like the puzzles of detective stories, is

[25] Isaac Asimov, *I, Robot*, Fawcett Crest, Greenwich, Conn., 1970 (1950), p. 6.

134

solved by ingenious application of the ground rules of the narrative world. Of course, since the narrative world of *I, Robot* has not only normal science but the Laws of Robotics, one should note that this highly dis-expected technology in a world created by a 1950s grapholect is more fantastic than an orthodox 1950s detective tale.

In a similar fashion, one would argue that *More Than Human*, because telepathy is more fantastic than technology, is more fantastic than *I, Robot*. More fantastic still is *Childhood's End*, of course. But science fiction gets more and more fantastic. In *City* by Clifford D. Simak (1952; International Fantasy Award for 1953), another composite novel, each of the stories adds yet another fantastic element (like intelligent ant life, talking dogs, and the fauna of Jupiter) to the narrative world. Because the ground rules must repeatedly expand in this way, rather than expand once only as in *Childhood's End*, we should place Simak's work further along our continuum than Clarke's. At the extreme, we would find Lindsay's *A Voyage to Arcturus*. As we have seen, this last book presents a world different from our own and the differences are apparent against the background of organized bodies of knowledge. But the differences come up so frequently (five primary colors contrasting with our own optics; physiological mutation; *sui generis* evolution) and so often reverse even themselves that this work is not only science fiction within our wider definition but a true Fantasy.

| Asimov | Sturgeon | Clarke | Simak | Lindsay |
|--------|----------|--------|-------|---------|
| (*I, Robot*) | (*More Than Human*) | (*Childhood's End*) | (*City*) | (*A Voyage to Arcturus*) |

→ Fantasy

This continuum shows the genre limits, in terms of their use of the fantastic, of science fiction works ranging from their least to their most fantastic possibilities. As we have already seen, knowing that a work uses the fantastic to a greater or lesser degree is often as critically useful as knowing the genre to which one would normally assign it. However, since placement on the continuum of the fantastic is made only on the basis of a work's use of the fantastic, we can use the continuum to suggest useful comparisons among works not in the same genre. We have seen that the works of Doyle belong to the left of Asimov and that Asimov's works might be thought of as irreducibly fantastic for science fiction by either of our definitions. However, detective tales do not always confine themselves to Doyle's use of the fantastic. Poe himself, in "Murders in the Rue Morgue," adds an extra and significant fantastic element, the homicidal ape. Similarly, in a work like Robert Bloch's *Psycho*, the mystery is only clarified when the fantastic becomes true, when we realize that the murderer and his mother are two parts of a highly dis-expected schizoid personality. Detective fiction, then, like science fiction, occupies not a point but a range along the continuum of the fantastic. At the extreme Fantasy end, we find a thriller like Cortázar's "Continuity of Parks" (pp. 39-41). If, for the sake of demonstration, we may consider the thriller, even the Fantasy thriller, as part of an expanded genre of detective fiction, then the continuum begins to look like this:

| science fiction | | Asimov (*I, Robot*) | Sturgeon (*More Than Human*) | Clarke (*Childhood's End*) | Simak (*City*) | Lindsay (*A Voyage to Arcturus*) | |
|---|---|---|---|---|---|---|---|
| detective fiction | Doyle ("The Speckled Band") | Bloch (*Psycho*) | | | | Cortázar ("Continuity of Parks") | → Fantasy |

We should be able to draw theoretical conclusions from an inspection of this image of the continuum.

First, let us note the gap between Bloch and Cortázar. One can find numerous works that satisfy our notion of detective fiction and still, by virtue of the continual dependence on the reversal of the ground rules of the narrative world, satisfy our definition of Fantasy. E. T. A. Hoffmann's "Mademoiselle de Scudéri" (1820) and Alain Robbe-Grillet's *The Erasers* (1953) are two such. It is difficult, however, to find detective fictions that are more fantastic than *Psycho* yet stop short of true Fantasy. One can easily hypothesize that many genres distribute their members along a range on the continuum of the fantastic; many of these ranges may overlap to a greater or lesser extent (as do those of detective and science fiction); and for many of these genres there may exist Fantasies not continuously related to the main range. This discontinuity gives rise to the urge to create a special genre for Fantasy even though most Fantasies (like those of Lindsay and Robbe-Grillet) belong equally to other genres defined by diverse principles.

On the other hand, the range of some other genres, like science fiction, are continuous up to and including Fantasy. This continuity explains some of the terminological dilemmas about Fantasy and many other genres (fairy tale, for instance) that seem associated with Fantasy yet are clearly not truly Fantasies. Thus, the pictorial representation of the continuum of the fantastic, even if it yields no other fruit, helps explain the ontology of the genre of Fantasy and the relation of that genre to the paradigmatic examples of other genres.

The second possibility the continuum should bring to mind is one of cross-generic comparison. We have found that placement along the continuum is a key factor in comparing *More Than Human* and *Childhood's End*. Conversely, in our earlier discussion of classical detective tales (see "The Fantastic and Perspective"), we were able to obviate problems in the choice of aesthetic dicta by carefully confining our inquiry to works by Poe, Doyle, and Chesterton that fell at the same point along the continuum. This suggests that comparison between works at the same point on the continuum, like those of Bloch and Asimov, might prove just as fruitful as comparison among works within a single traditional genre. There are many areas in which the diversity of genre-defining principles causes more confusion than it yields illumination. Application of the continuum of the fantastic may help bring order out of such a situation.

*Childhood's End* is certainly science fiction, but it is also just as certainly utopian fiction. The main point of the book is that man will achieve a perfectly unified society (by means of telepathy) when he changes his basic nature, a change that is possible. Indeed, although Clarke cannot promise that Overlords will come to nursemaid us through our atomic crises, his book may still encourage political restraint for the sake of man's more wonderful future. In this regard, Clarke's vision is much like that of Edward Bellamy, author of America's most influential utopia, *Looking Backward 2000–1887* (1888). Bellamy conceived of "state capitalism" emerging inevitably when the inability of private enterprise to cope with labor troubles forced government into buying more and more industry.

> No business is so essentially the public business as the industry and commerce on which people's livelihood depends. . . . the whole mass of the people was behind it.[26]

Just as the inevitable biological change in Clarke's book yields new people fitted for telepathic communal living, so in Bellamy's tract the advent of the new economic order so changes the human attitude toward work that, "In their lucid intervals, even our insane are eager to do what they

[26] Edward Bellamy, *Looking Backward*, Houghton Mifflin, Boston, 1926 (1888), pp. 56-57.

can."[27] Both books make wide use of technology. In *Childhood's End* technology is both a threat to the existence of man and the tool by which he is restrained; in *Looking Backward*, full of nineteenth-century optimism, technology provides the material largesse that releases man's better nature. In both cases, the technology represented is, in context, fantastic: Karellen subdues the whole earth by his show of force and future Boston's distribution system of pneumatic tubes is "certainly perfect."[28] Though normally assigned to two different genres, both these works treat human nature, social organization, and technology in parallel fantastic ways. From the standpoint of their use of the fantastic, they are quite properly classed together.

Attention to the use these works make of the fantastic helps reveal literary relationships made obscure by conventional genre distinctions. Such attention can also help us explore distinctions within the single genre of utopian fiction. William Morris wrote *News From Nowhere* in part as an alternative to what he derisively called Bellamy's "Cockney paradise."[29] Where Bellamy projects his society into an avowed future, Morris chooses a future that he calls "fourteenth century"[30] in its restfulness and its full integration of the activities of life; where Bellamy depends for his change in human nature on a wide material base produced by highly developed technology, Morris imagines a human change arising from making work artful and thereby obviating the need for enslaving machines; where Bellamy sees social perfection in the centralized "industrial army,"[31] Morris says "we discourage centralization all we can."[32] Each writer

---

[27] *Ibid.*, p. 131.    [28] *Ibid.*, p. 107.
[29] William Morris, *News From Nowhere*, James Redmond, ed., Routledge & Kegan Paul, London, 1970, p. xxxvii.
[30] *Ibid.*, p. 36.
[31] Bellamy, *Looking Backward*, pp. 128ff.
[32] Morris, *News From Nowhere*, p. 57.

addresses himself to the contemporary views of history, technology, and human nature; each treats these areas fantastically. However, in extrapolating, rather than reversing, the perspective on technology, Bellamy is somewhat less fantastic than Morris. Put another way, Bellamy's book, like *Childhood's End*, is science fiction; Morris' "vision," which abandons, rather than differing from, contemporary technology, is not. Morris, the more fantastic, gives a more thorough alternative to contemporary perspectives, and thus creates a more unified work. This unity in the use he makes of the fantastic explains in part why *News From Nowhere* is both more critically acclaimed and more enduring than *Looking Backward*. By examining their use of the fantastic, these three works of utopian and science fiction can cast light on each other in ways that complement the inquiries of conventional genre criticism.

The word "utopia" literally means "no-place," but when Thomas More coined it in 1516, he also meant it to pun on "eu-topia," meaning "good-place." By analogy, we often call a work that projects a future bad society a "dystopia," meaning "bad-place." In other words, the genre of utopias contains both utopias and dystopias. This is a slight terminological confusion, but one so well established in genre criticism that it is difficult to overcome it. We might wish to note that those works of the genre *utopias* which really are eu-topias present societies that seem to carry the author's approval, while dystopias seem to carry the author's disapproval. *The Time Machine* is a dystopia.

When Wells' Time Traveller first arrives in the future by a fantastic reversal of the laws of classical physics, he finds elegant, childlike people of leisure. The first impression is one of a pastoral utopia, a vision not unlike Morris'. However, when the Time Traveller talks with these strange folk, he quickly discovers that they are morons. We learn that their mental and physical degeneration into a new kind of human being has come about by natural selection maximizing those characteristics that favor satisfactory survival in a world devoid of useful labor. In thus stressing the importance of labor to a truly human utopia, Wells reveals himself as a successor to Morris. However, unlike Morris, his work is based not on a fantastic reversal of the perspective of historical determinism but on an orthodox historical extrapolation of the role of technology in society. By extrapolating the notion of increasing reliance on technology, Wells is unlike Morris, but quite like Bellamy. Bellamy's Julian West arrives in the future by a means quite as fantastic as time travel; while in a hypnotic sleep, a strange confluence of atmospheric effects allows him to survive in suspended animation. *The Time Machine* and *Looking Backward* are, from the standpoint of their use of the fantastic and their use of technological extrapolation, quite comparable. However, Bellamy clearly approves of his imagined society, while Wells disapproves of his. Despite Wells' disapproval, however, *The Time Machine* is like both *Looking Backward* and *Childhood's End* in at least one significant regard: they are all works of science fiction.

Wells' dystopia fulfills our general definition for the genre of science fiction by presenting a narrative world whose difference from our own is apparent in comparison with an organized body of knowledge. There is no reason, however, that a utopia must proceed in this fashion. A work like *News From Nowhere*, although it completely reverses certain Victorian perspectives, especially the perspective on history, does not reverse, or even create a highly disexpected version of, an organized body of knowledge. In similar fashion, David Karp's *One* (1953) is a *Brave New World* kind of dystopia that eschews the technology of bugging and the linguistic reversals of Newspeak but creates just as chilling a world of controlled minds by extrapolating man's desire to gain approval, at any moral cost, by informing on his neighbors. This dystopia extrapolates not from an organized body of knowledge, such as modern sociology, but from a number of prevalent though unarticulated social perspectives. These perspectives (most visible perhaps in the notorious child-parent dilemmas that arose in Nazi Germany) almost completely reverse contemporary perspectives on the methods and purposes of democratic governments. If Karp's Benevolent State, with its Department of Internal Examination, does not seem fantastic today, we must remember that in 1953 most of the world still called the concentration camps "unthinkable." However, regardless of where a reader feels *One* falls on the continuum of the fantastic, it is clearly a non-science fiction dystopia based on extrapolation, just as *News From Nowhere* is a non-science fiction utopia based on reversal: both works deal not with an organized body of knowledge but with a more amorphous collection of ideas one might call contemporary perspectives.

To complete our dissection of the genre of utopias, we should note that so far we have made use of three criteria in distinguishing works within the genre:

1. Does the narrative world seem to have the author's approval?
2. Is the work an extrapolation or a reversal of contemporary ideas?
3. Do those ideas recall an organized body of knowledge, or are they an unstructured collection of contemporary perspectives?

Permuting these dichotomies yields eight categories. We have already described works that fall within five of these.

One can easily find works that fulfill the requirements of the other three sub-genres. Rabelais' "Abbey of Thélème" is a famous utopia based on the simple extrapolation of the contemporary perspectives on gentility: if properly noble and beautiful people were admitted to it, the abbey would automatically be a utopia when run by the single rule, "Do what thou wilt." This work is a utopia based on an extrapolation of contemporary perspectives. George Orwell's *Animal Farm*, like *One*, is a dystopia that extrapolates certain dismal perspectives on human nature. However, by extrapolating these contemporary perspectives not into the future but into an animal fable, Orwell bases his world on at least one reversal: that the unhuman becomes the human. (In this regard, Orwell's fable belongs on the continuum of the fantastic with other animal fables even though they are not in the genre of utopias.) Eugene Zamiatin's *We* (1924) is an early science fiction dystopia: in this United State, where all people are known as numbers and "I" is a forbidden concept, all ideas of political science are reversed and technology expands to include an operation for "the surgical removal of fancy,"[33] which gives final victory to the dictator. Adding these three works to the five we have already discussed, we can display pictorially the internal structure of the genre of utopias as revealed by our three distinctions.

The diagram organizes the relations among works solely within the genre of utopias. (The parenthetical numbers will be useful at a later stage in our discussion.) Note that, by this scheme, half the categories of utopian fiction, the lower half, fall also within the genre of science fiction. Note that each distinction is potentially important in deciding how fantastic a work is. Note also that works may be profitably compared by this scheme across generic boundaries

[33] Eugene Zamiatin, *We*, Dutton, New York, 1952 (1924), p. 167.

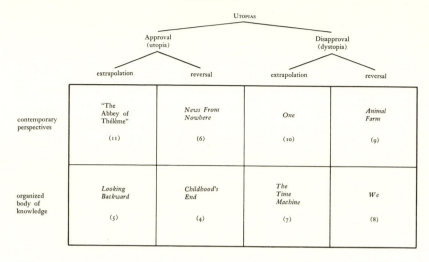

if they share a use of the fantastic, or within a generic boundary even if they do not. By trying to consider the uses made of the fantastic, we have developed a scheme of relationships to complement normal genre study.

This type of study could be applied whenever genres have significant overlap on the continuum of the fantastic. Perhaps the most significant genre that so overlaps with utopian fiction is satire. Gilbert Highet's excellent *Anatomy of Satire* is a book-length study offering an exhaustive description of the internal structure of this genre. For our purposes, perhaps, it would serve as well to note merely the confluent characteristics that Highet attributes to satire: topical, realistic, shocking, informal, funny. By the first two of these terms, Highet intends to remind us that satire talks to a particular time, the satirist's time, and pulls no punches: "all satirists are at heart idealists."[34] Satirists hold up to ridicule contemporary situations that fall short of

[34] Gilbert Highet, *The Anatomy of Satire*, Princeton University Press, Princeton, New Jersey, 1962, p. 243.

144

their ideals. This ridicule is what makes satires less than formal, for ridicule is untamed. And, if done right, ridicule is shocking and funny as well.

Almost all utopian literature, either by proposing a superior alternative to our world or by showing how our world is going wrong, measures our world against an ideal and flirts with satire.

> The central problem of satire is its relation to reality. Satire wishes to expose and criticize and shame human life, but it pretends to tell the whole truth and nothing but the truth . . . either by showing an apparently factual but really ludicrous and debased picture of this world; or by showing a picture of another world, with which our world is contrasted.[35]

If the debased world is an animal fable in which man is inferior to beasts, the work is as likely to be *Animal Farm* as Gulliver's "Voyage to the Houyhnhnms"; if in the completely other world, we must find happiness by tending our own gardens, the work is as likely to be *News From Nowhere* as Voltaire's *Candide*. Of course, much utopian fiction is not satiric. *One*, for instance, is not funny; "The Abbey of Thélème" does not criticize contemporary people for not all being of high birth (though *Gargantua and Pantagruel* as a whole is clearly satiric). Utopian fiction, then, overlaps with the genre of satire. Bellamy wrote, just two years after the organization of the American Federation of Labor, that competitive capitalism led to a situation where

> In fact, it had come to be the exceptional thing to see any class of laborers pursue their avocation steadily for more than a few months at a time.[36]

[35] *Ibid.*, pp. 158-59.
[36] Bellamy, *Looking Backward*, p. 15.

And Morris tells us that in those decentralized future times, people referred to "the Parliament House, or Dung Market."[37] Even though *Childhood's End* may create its alternative world with the seriousness of gospel, some works of utopian fiction may be utterly satiric.

Satire is inherently fantastic. Not only does it depend on narrative worlds that reverse the perspectives of the world outside the narrative, but the style usually depends on irony, "stating the reverse of the truth as though it were clear truth."[38] Such structural reversal is at the heart of science fiction as a genre and at the heart of utopian literature as a genre. It is small wonder that these three genres overlap. Zamiatin gives us many passages that are equally satiric, dystopic, and science fictional. In the following, the Operation Department is the branch of government that is entrusted with performing political lobotomies and finally develops the operation for the removal of fancy:

> About five centuries ago, when the work of the Operation Department was only beginning, there were yet to be found some fools who compared our Operation Department with the ancient Inquisition. But this is as absurd as to compare a surgeon performing a tracheotomy with a highway cutthroat. Both use a knife, perhaps the same kind of knife, both do the same thing, viz., cut the throat of a living man; yet one is a welldoer, the other is a murderer; one is marked plus, the other minus. . . . All this becomes perfectly clear in one second, in one turn of our wheel of logic, the teeth of which engage that *minus*, turn it upward, and thus change its aspect.[39]

[37] Morris, *News From Nowhere*, p. 34.
[38] Highet, *The Anatomy of Satire*, p. 61.
[39] Zamiatin, *We*, p. 77.

This direct reversal of minus to plus or plus to minus is the
fundamental structural stimulus for the affect of the fantastic. It is as likely to be found in satire as in utopian fiction or
science fiction. In a sense, these three overlapping genres
together form a super-genre. We can represent this super-
genre, including the detail of the sub-genres of utopian fiction, in a single display.

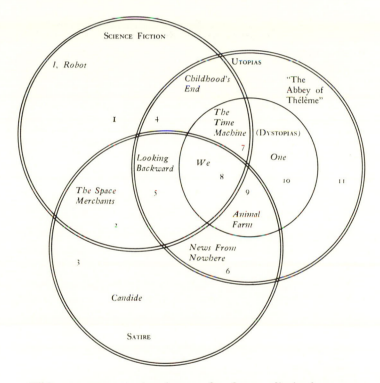

This super-genre contains works along a limited segment
of the continuum of the fantastic. Although we have been
able to distinguish *Childhood's End* as more fantastic than
*I, Robot*, both are more fantastic than a Sherlock Holmes

147

story and much more fantastic than a novel by Henry James. Allowing a super-genre to draw from a segment, rather than a point, on the continuum, we are less likely to omit works that may well illuminate each other and our study. The diagram represents pictorially the notion that each of the three genres might or might not overlap with either or both of the other two. *The Space Merchants*,[40] which satirizes advertising in an overpopulated future, is one of numerous works that fall in area 2, a classification that we have not discussed but that our theoretical notions of the fantastic and its functioning predict should exist. Similarly, *Candide* is noted as one of countless members of area 3, those works that are satiric but do not fall in the genres of utopian or science fiction. Note that dystopias fall completely within the genre of utopias, thus continuing the time-honored terminological confusion, though representing the structure of the genre clearly.

If one refers again to the display of categories within the genre of utopian fiction (p. 144), one sees that the parenthetical numbers correspond to the position of works on the map of the super-genre. There is no theoretical reason why a utopian work that reverses an organized body of knowledge (*Childhood's End*) cannot be satiric. It just happens, however, that Clarke's novel is not. Were a novel to occupy the category of *Childhood's End* but in addition be satiric, it would to that extent be more fantastic than Clarke's novel. (Heinlein's *Stranger in a Strange Land* is such a work.) In other words, it would be further right on the continuum. Our map of the super-genre includes works keyed to those on the display of utopian fiction in order to show that both pictorial summaries arise from a consideration of

[40] Frederik Pohl and C. M. Kornbluth, *The Space Merchants*, Ballantine, New York, 1972 (1953).

148

the nature of the fantastic; both have reference to the continuum of the fantastic; and both may complement each other quite as well as they complement normal genre criticism.

In addition to showing new relationships among works that use the fantastic to similar degrees, inspection of each display alone may well be profitable. For example, works in areas 4 and 7 seem to assume that man will change under the operation of science, while works in areas 6 and 9 seem to assume that society will change under the operation of man. This contrast suggests two hypotheses: 1) science fiction writers feel man is ultimately subject to powers beyond his control, while 2) satirists feel that men are always responsible for their actions. These hypotheses are borne out in two ways. First, works in area 1 inevitably show science as determining man's fate, while works in area 3 invariably call man to task for failing to meet an ideal. Second, a hybrid work still in the genre of utopias, such as *Looking Backward* in area 5, seems to hold a line between man's making his society good and society's making man good. This dialectic represents well the combination of attitudes of a fantastic work near the center of this super-genre.

In "The Fantastic and Perspective" we saw that a consideration of the use of the fantastic could complement the normal study of worldview, regardless of the genre using the fantastic. In this chapter, we see how, regardless of worldview, we can use the fantastic to address questions of genre. We can use the consideration of the fantastic to arrange all narratives along a continuum; we can use this continuum to help establish the internal structure of a genre or build up the structure of a super-genre that represents a segment of that continuum. Such structures can interilluminate genre questions or independently suggest new insights in genre criticism. By capitalizing on the idea that science fiction, utopian fiction, and satire may all be fantastic in similar ways, all parts of a single super-genre, we see how a consideration of the way works use the fantastic can produce new analytic insights that complement the products of normal genre criticism.

# ℣

# The Fantastic and Literary History

LITERARY history has two main branches. Extra-textual literary history concerns itself with the growth of the reading public, the laws governing stage performance, the biographies of authors, and so on. Intra-textual literary history concerns itself with the development of those realms whose analysis depends upon examination of individual texts: the growth and development of genres, the modifications of worldview, the evolution of grapholects, and so on. We have already seen that a consideration of the uses works make of the fantastic complements normal synchronic study of these phenomena. This chapter will attempt to demonstrate how an historical application of the same considerations would complement the usual inquiries of intra-textual literary history.

Over a period of time, perspectives change. This was the case for Walter Scott's unfortunate great-aunt who found she could no longer read Aphra Behn; this is the case for whole cultures. Most of Victorian England, until the 1890s, saw technology as a threat to the quality of life. The spread of industrialism was likened to cancer; London was called "the great Wen." Even Dickens, the first English novelist to so absorb the new technological age that he could use it as the world of a novel, still used naturalistic metaphor in describing that technology. In the Coketown of *Hard Times* (1854), "the piston of the steam-engine worked monotonously up and down, like the head of an elephant in a state of melancholy madness."[1] Dickens, however, is also the first novelist to use technology as the vehicle, rather than the tenor, of a metaphor. In Thomas Gradgrind's school, the children have numbers instead of names, and Gradgrind himself

seemed a cannon loaded to the muzzle with facts, and prepared to blow them clean out of the regions of childhood at one discharge. He seemed a galvanizing apparatus, too, charged with a grim mechanical substitute for the tender young imaginations that were to be stormed away.[2]

In this shift from tenor to vehicle, we see the first breeze of a change in perspectives that was to blow away the world of Victoria.

We see a similar stylistic shift in post-World-War-I America. Hemingway sought a road back to a pastoral, or even wilderness, rejuvenation in "Big Two-Hearted River" (1925): "From the time he had gotten down off the train and the baggage man had thrown his pack out of the open car door things had been different."[3] The technology, the war, even the railroad's cinders, had burnt the wilderness. And broken the man. The wilderness courage of Natty Bumpo fails Nick Adams, and he cannot fish the swamp for that would be "tragic."[4] Richard Brautigan has already absorbed the world in which this failure is foredestined. In *Trout Fishing In America* (1967), the narrator again wants to find rejuvenation, and, like Nick Adams, he cannot. But notice that in Brautigan's style, nature is now metaphorized by technology:

[1] Charles Dickens, *Hard Times*, Holt, Rinehart and Winston, New York, 1958 (1854), p. 20.
[2] *Ibid.*, p. 3.
[3] Ernest Hemingway, *In Our Time*, Charles Scribner's Sons, New York, 1958 (1925), p. 179.
[4] *Ibid.*, p. 211.

. . . that creek turned out to be a real son-of-a-bitch.
. . . the canyon was so narrow the creek poured out like
water from a faucet. . . .
   You had to be a plumber to fish that creek.
   After that first trout I was alone in there. But I didn't
know it until later.[5]

A metaphor, like the fantastic, depends on the rapid and
direct reversal of some perspective. "That man was a lion
in battle" depends for its effectiveness on our first understanding that a man is definitely *not* a lion.[6] Metaphors, of
course, do not reconfigure the ground rules of the narrative
world; they embellish it and give it its tone. But the creation—and adoption—of a tone is the first step toward the
adoption of a new perspective. In *In Our Time* Hemingway,
trying to escape technology, adopts the tone of defeat;
Brautigan operates in a technologically dominated world.
Dickens embellishes with technological metaphor; Wells
can create a new technological world. Stylistic developments are the paragraphs in literary history; changes in the
uses of the fantastic are the chapters.
   Coming after Dickens, and being himself a student of science, Wells creates the scientific romance, a new genre
based on the application of mechanism to man. He agreed
with his teacher, T. H. Huxley, that "the principle of mechanism" was "the central hypothesis of modern biology."[7]
Like any good Victorian, Wells' first use of this interiorized
sense of mechanism was to show how mechanism itself
would destroy humanity. Hence, *The Time Machine* (1895).

[5] Richard Brautigan, *Trout Fishing In America*, Delta, New York,
1967, p. 19.
[6] For the relation between structure in style and in other levels
of narration, see Eric S. Rabkin, *Narrative Suspense*, University of
Michigan Press, Ann Arbor, 1973, chapters 1 and 2.
[7] Herbert L. Sussman, *Victorians and the Machine*, Harvard University Press, Cambridge, Mass., 1968, p. 135.

However, Wells was a scientist by training, and this led him to economic determinism in politics. The combination of these two made it possible for Wells to create not only a technological dystopia, but technological utopias. Before 1900, Wells' literary attitude toward science is ambivalent.

For every selfless investigator of nature's secrets, there is a mad scientist. The well-intentioned time-explorer is matched by Griffen, the homicidal scientist of the *Invisible Man.*[8]

After 1900 this ambivalence disappears.

Kenneth Burke asserts that reality is a matter not so much of how things are as how we think they are; not of what things do but of what we expect them to do; not of actuality but of conception.[9] Just as Scott's great-aunt found her world changed, because her perspectives had changed, so H. G. Wells found his ambivalence had passed away with the nineteenth century. Perhaps it was his politics working on his ethics, perhaps it was the prosperity of Victorian expansion, perhaps it was a greater familiarity with a technological life; whatever the cause, Wells is the first English utopian who does not need to escape a technological world. In *A Modern Utopia* (1905) Wells leaves his dire warnings far behind and begins his career of energetic social planning, a career that culminates in the enthusiastically militaristic work, *The Shape of Things to Come* (1933). In the former utopia, Wells tames his own Victorian need to escape technology by creating a non-scientist ruling elite; by the time of the latter utopia, Wells is able to recommend a world run by the benevolent despotism of the engineers.

As Wells developed, and as England moved from 1854 to

---

[8] *Ibid.*, p. 163.
[9] Kenneth Burke, *Permanence and Change*, Bobbs-Merrill, Indianapolis, 1965 (1954, 1935), p. 22.

1933, technology did not pose a lesser threat to man; the machine did not fail before the assaults of the garden; human happiness did not flourish in sweat shops. But human views of technology did change: the embellishment of metaphor became the escape of the fantastic and, finally, the vision of paradise. By the time of *The Shape of Things to Come*, we have already passed into the world of *The Jungle* (1906) in which man is not only slave to the machine but eaten by it and spit out again to be eaten by other men as sausage; yet the machine had become so familiar an element of daily life, and so vital to man's new-found modes of self-expression, that only a fool would escape it. In the twentieth century, all utopian schemes have included technology, and it is only since the emergence of the psychic monolith of The Bomb that utopias are required to include, as Wells did with his ruling elite of humanists, a safeguard against technology gone astray. Our fantastic worlds directly reflect the worlds in which we live.

Although Wells is often referred to as the first scientifically trained writer in English,[10] this is not so. Arthur Conan Doyle was a trained physician, and only when he failed to achieve a sufficient income from his seaside practice did he turn to the production of fiction. While Wells was still predicting the perverse evolution of post-human monsters in 1895, Doyle had already created in 1887 (*A Study in Scarlet*) the figure of the curative, all-powerful, rationalist: Sherlock Holmes. Holmes, as we have pointed out, offered two escapes: the consolation of the puzzle and the distribution of justice. One must also note that the agent of these escapes is a prototypical scientist, a dispassionate observer of minutiae who constructs hypotheses, tests them, and explains away the mysterious. While Wells and most of England still found science ambivalent at best,

---

[10] Sussman, *Victorians*, p. 163.

Doyle adopted the perspectives of science without a qualm, and in so doing helped change the perspective of a nation. While Wells used the scientific to chasten, Doyle used the scientific to cure. In comparing these fantastic worlds, we see the interrelation of genres in the development of utopian fiction during the tumultuous early years of this century.

We confined our earlier examination of detective fiction to a comparatively stable time in the growth of English culture. Within this period we found that the relative proportions of the escape of the puzzle and the escape of justice shifted: the puzzle became less important, justice became more important. Still, there was always a combination of the two escapes, and both were offered simultaneously through the agency of the great detective. We can examine in more detail how a genre develops historically by examining detective fictions written outside this stable period.

Agatha Christie, with more than 400,000,000 copies of her works sold, is clearly a dominant voice in the field of detective fiction. In *The A.B.C. Murders* (1936) we meet Hercule Poirot, Agatha's answer to Sherlock Holmes, the Great Detective, the intellectual, rational Belgian, who is the most famed crime-solver in England. Most of the story is the first person narration of Captain Hastings, Poirot's not-too-bright, always-noting-the-obvious companion. A few small chapters are inserted in the book and labelled "(Not From Captain Hastings' Personal Narrative)." These chapters, largely concerning a born loser named Alexander Bonaparte Cust, give the reader access to information hidden from Poirot and Hastings. The book presents us with a puzzle: who is committing a bizarre series of murders? Ultimately, Poirot not only solves this puzzle, but in so doing distributes justice. However, unlike Father Brown,

Poirot does not distribute justice in the name of a higher good; he distributes it only as a by-product of solving the puzzle. Agatha Christie's puzzles are as complex and unlikely as Chesterton's, but in the work of the post-war writer, as in the work of Poe, the solution of a puzzle provides the dominant escape.

A fiction, like a puzzle, is artificially constructed to lead to some sort of resolution. After World War I, perhaps because of the devastation that that cataclysm wrought on Victorian optimism, Chestertonian faith became nearly impossible to maintain in any narrative world too strongly resembling our own. It is small wonder then that detective fictions, to justify the distribution of justice, began to elaborate their fictional worlds in more complex and self-reflexively literary puzzles. In *The A.B.C. Murders*, we find an orthographic series of murders that follows the mindless alphabetic pattern of a children's game: the first murder occurs in Andover, the victim is Alice Ascher; the second murder occurs in Bexhill-on-Sea, the victim is Betty Barnard; the third murder occurs in Churston, the victim is Sir Carmichael Clarke. Each murder is preceded by a letter sent to Poirot by someone who signs himself A.B.C., gives the date and place of the next crime, and challenges the great detective to stop him.

The world of this novel is in some senses a fairy tale world governed by laws that, though they permit evil, work ultimately to the good of man. Though surely Christie knew of the random murder of Bobby Franks by Leopold and Loeb in 1924, she still has Poirot say in this 1936 novel: " '. . . there isn't such a thing as a murderer who commits crimes at random.' "[11] This must have been, in a world that had seen

[11] Agatha Christie, *The A.B.C. Murders*, Dodd, Mead, New York, 1936, p. 110.

157

The Great War and the Great Depression, a very comforting assertion—especially coming from the one figure most in control of the narrative world.

> "If we knew the exact reason—fantastic, perhaps, to us —but logical to him—of *why* our madman commits these crimes, we should know, perhaps, who the next victim is likely to be."[12]

The puzzle merely requires that we understand the thinking of a madman, and then all will be sane.

The reader may well have come to think, from his private information, that Alexander Bonaparte Cust is A.B.C. Cust is a reclusive epileptic who is always in the murder city on the date of the crime; a typewriter is found in his room that matches the one used to type the letters sent to Poirot; and so forth. A bizarre web of connections, too long to recount here, points convincingly to A. B. Cust, who is apprehended in Doncaster after the murder of the fourth victim, George Earlsfield. Scotland Yard is satisfied; Hastings is satisfied; perhaps even the reader is satisfied. The murderer is known. All the clues fit.

However, early in the book, Poirot reveals his variation from the classical literary norm by satirizing Sherlock Holmes and, incidentally, warning Hastings against "the clue":

> "Well?" I demanded eagerly.
> . . .
> "The crime," said Poirot, "was committed by a man of medium height with red hair and a cast in the left eye. He limps slightly on the right foot and has a mole just below the shoulder-blade."
> "Poirot?" I cried.

[12] *Ibid.*, p. 112.

For a moment I was completely taken in. Then the twinkle in my friend's eye undeceived me.

. . .

"*Mon ami*, what will you? You fix upon me a look of doglike devotion and demand of me a pronouncement à la Sherlock Holmes! Now for the truth—*I do not know what the murderer looks like, nor where he lives, nor how to set hands upon him.*"

"If only he had left some clue," I murmured.

"Yes, the clue—it is always the clue that attracts you. Alas that he did not smoke the cigarette and leave the ash, and then step in it with a shoe that has nails of a curious pattern. No—he is not so obliging. . . ."[13]

This little speech demonstrates Christie's great skill at manipulating reader affect within the confining conventions of her genre. By making light of Holmes, Christie subliminally tells us that hers is no simple fairy tale world. However, by using this very speech to further build Poirot's good sense in comparison to those around him, Christie lets us know at a deeper level that, however complex it may be, this is still a fairy tale world after all with Poirot the presiding genius. By seeming to admit chaos into life, Christie is able to create a narrative world that is not in the least chaotic.

On the contrary, this narrative world is orthographic. We *expect* that the murders will follow the alphabetic series. And we expect, when Poirot is dissatisfied, that his dissatisfaction is based on a true understanding of "crime" as committed in a literary landscape. Beside each victim's body is found a railway schedule opened to the page giving the trains from the murder town. These schedules, listing towns alphabetically, are known as *A.B.C. Guides*. They are the

[13] *Ibid.*, pp. 59-60.

only Hastings-type clues found, clues that are easy to grasp, but, as Poirot points out, clues that are deceptive: they do not reveal the murderer because they are planted by the murderer. All of this is obvious in a book where the clues are books.

Cust is in custody; everyone is satisfied. But still Poirot, trying to account for every piece in the puzzle, says that, " 'Until I get at the reason for those letters being written to me, I shall not feel that the case is solved.' "[14] Poirot's sense of formal incompletion prompts him to further investigation. It is discovered that Cust is the dupe of Franklin Clarke. Cust can be fooled just because he is a man used to losing and because he is an epileptic who can't account to himself for his actions during his fits. Franklin has constructed an elaborate frame of deception so that the murder motive will appear to be related to a particular mania, whereas in actuality the idea of a series was merely to keep the murder of Sir Carmichael Clarke from garnering special attention. That murder was the only one that mattered to Franklin, the murder that would allow him to inherit. By solving this obscure puzzle, by not snatching at the ready solution, Poirot not only apprehends the actual murderer, but frees the poor duped Cust. Thus is the puzzle solved and justice distributed simultaneously by the great detective.

In this fiction, however, the distribution of justice is really a by-product of the ornate game meant to satisfy readers too familiar with the genre's conventions. Indeed, from its inception, the whole series of murders has more the appearance of literature than life. After receiving the first letter, Poirot asks Hastings what kind of crime he would like if he could have one to order for the pair to investigate. Hastings

14 *Ibid.*, p. 251.

gives a parody of a detective story that nonetheless turns out to describe *The A.B.C. Murders* very well.[15] Poirot says, " 'You have made there a very pretty resume of nearly all the detective stories that have ever been written.' " Yet, despite this warning against the literary, the conversation of the two friends gradually loses touch with its human basis, the threat of murder, and lapses into the playful. " 'I admit,' [Hastings] said, 'that a second murder in a book often cheers things up.' "[16]

Eliade writes that

Objects or acts acquire a value, and in so doing become real, because they participate, after one fashion or another, in a reality that transcends them.[17]

To a reader of detective fiction, that transcendent reality is the solvable literary puzzle. Poirot and Hastings merely participate in our own reader reality when they view murder not as crime and sin but as a source of cheer. While in Chesterton the puzzle is the mere occasion for justice, in Agatha Christie justice is the minimal justification for interest in the puzzle. Human suffering, theology, and ethics are truncated as the importance of the puzzle—and literary reality itself—becomes more important. Increasing self-reflection marks the historic development of the genre of detective fiction after World War I.

Perhaps the best-known modern detective tale is Agatha Christie's *And Then There Were None* (1940). In this work, ten people are marooned on Indian Island. In the room of each is a children's nursery rhyme beginning, "Ten little Indian boys went out to dine; / One choked his little

---

[15] *Ibid.*, p. 16.    [16] *Ibid.*, p. 17.
[17] Mircea Eliade, *Cosmos and History*, Willard R. Trask, transl., Harper & Row, New York, 1959 (1949), pp. 3-4.

self and then there were nine."[18] The rhyme proceeds until we find "One little Indian boy left all alone; / He went and hanged himself and then there were none." Although in sight of the Devon coast,

> There was something magical about an island—the mere word suggested fantasy. You lost touch with the world—an island was a world of its own. A world, perhaps, from which you might never return. He thought: I'm leaving my ordinary life behind me.[19]

The island, like a book, was both fantastic and self-contained. One by one, in circumstances that ape those of the rhyme, the inhabitants are found murdered. As their cohorts are killed, the survivors mull over their situation. In a clever contraposition of the old saw, "Truth is stranger than fiction," one of the characters says of their predicament that " 'It's easier of belief than the truth!' "[20] Like her earlier book then, *And Then There Were None* offers Christie's readers a fairy tale world, shaped and proceeding according to the rules of a children's game, resulting in a series of murders, and engaging us primarily not in the ethical questions of killing but in the puzzle of seeking the killer.

Unlike *The A.B.C. Murders*, this later book does not have a great detective. Instead, the narrative uses free indirect style to close in on the thoughts of each of the characters while we readers try, along with the dwindling number of survivors, to solve the mystery. Since there is no great detective, perhaps we do not feel the lack of justice. In fact, the ten murders proceed inexorably to their conclusion with

[18] Agatha Christie, *And Then There Were None*, Dodd, Mead, New York, 1940, Pocket Books, New York, 1972, p. 28. (Page references are to Pocket Books edition.)

[19] *Ibid.*, p. 29.                    [20] *Ibid.*, p. 77.

the mystery still unsolved. There is a minimal attempt at distribution of justice; each of the victims has in some way, by some act of omission, been involved in the death of someone else. " 'It explains Indian Island. There are crimes that cannot be brought home to their perpetrators.' "[21] These were " 'cases that the law couldn't touch.' "[22] But the moral notion that these people all deserved death without jury, or deserved death at all, is never explored. Instead, all die; our major involvement is in figuring out who did the killing; and our ethical sense is short-circuited by attention to the arcane puzzle. After the last of the ten dies, the book shifts to Scotland Yard. The Assistant Commissioner says, " 'The whole thing's fantastic—impossible. Ten people killed on a bare rock of an island—and we don't know who did it, or why, or how.' "[23]

As is the case in the classic detective tale, the fantastic in this novel is naturalized: following the mystery comes the explanation. The explanation, however, comes not from the deduction of a great detective but from the confession, found in a floating bottle, of the murderer. It would be unkind to those who have not read this classic to explain the mystery. What one should note, however, is that the explanation itself, with no one captured, no distribution of justice, no punishment of the murderer, is the *only* resolution offered the reader by the ending of the book. The classic detective fiction offers a two-pronged escape; *And Then There Were None* offers the literarily purer single escape of the solved puzzle, the perfect fitting of one fantastic piece to another to create a self-consistent fantastic world with no reference to the pain and ambiguity that murder implies in the world outside the book. By making the literary, fairy tale, and childlike elements of detective fiction more prominent, and by deemphasizing the role of the de-

[21] *Ibid.*, p. 72.       [22] *Ibid.*, p. 159.       [23] *Ibid.*, p. 160.

tective, Agatha Christie made a significant adaptation of the genre of detective fiction to a world that still wants its escapes, but has learned that those escapes can neither be too simple nor be expected to restore justice.

In the years following, in part because of the continuing assault on faith which was World War II, and in part because of the power of Agatha Christie's own formulas, the genre began to revitalize the great detective, but, to do this, justice had to be further deemphasized and the literary, formulaic, play qualities of the puzzle had to be further strengthened. As the conventions of a genre become better known to its reader, new works in a genre must become more and more fantastic in order to produce the same affect. If these fantastic elements are plot episodes, then the work tends toward the thriller, the supernatural tale, and so forth, all genres which have developed strongly and added inventive new gore to their repertories since World War II. Detective fiction, however, is predicated on the notion that the world is an ordered place. The supernatural is excluded. Someone benevolent is in control and no witch casts a spell that doesn't ultimately do good. If one cannot exaggerate content, then one must exaggerate form. After World War II, driven to more fantastic writing, the detective tale became more self-reflexive, more concerned with its own ontology as fiction. Among mainstream writers of detective fiction, Ellery Queen best exemplifies this movement to incorporate the fantastic.

Frederick Dannay and Manfred Lee were both born in 1905. Together, they wrote under the name Ellery Queen. If one likes, one can credit this fictional pseudonym with a life, a biography. Born in 1905, Ellery Queen published his first detective story in 1929. He has, since 1941, edited *Ellery Queen's Mystery Magazine*.[24] In 1953, Ellery Queen

---

[24] James D. Hart, ed., *The Oxford Companion to American Literature*, 4th ed., Oxford University Press, New York, 1965, p. 691.

published *The Scarlet Letters*. The hero of this obviously allusive tale is the detective, named Ellery Queen. Queen the hero is a successful writer of detective fiction, and editor of *Ellery Queen's Mystery Magazine*. He is drawn into the case by Nikki, his literary secretary, who fears for the life of her friend Martha. Martha is rich and married to Dirk Lawrence, whom she loves, but who is very jealous. In addition, Lawrence is an unsuccessful writer of mystery stories. The book is rife with references to Hawthorne, Poe, Brontë, and other cases of Ellery Queen. The characters all have something to do with fictional worlds: Martha is a Broadway producer; her suspected lover, Van Harrison, is an actor; and so on. Nikki goes to live with the Lawrences, presumably to help Dirk in his writing. While there, she sees that Martha is getting letters typed in red. Nikki realizes that whereas Hawthorne wrote a *novel* about a scarlet letter, this is *real*. Except that it isn't, since this is a novel written by Ellery Queen. But Ellery Queen is real too. In fact, while Ellery is tailing Martha, in order to remain unobtrusive, he "walked over to the news-stand and began to finger a copy of *Ellery Queen's Mystery Magazine*."[25] This is fantastic in the same way that *Through the Looking Glass* is fantastic when Alice doesn't know if she's in the red king's dream or vice versa. This self-reflection on its own existence as written artifact makes *The Scarlet Letters* the most fantastic detective story we have so far examined.

Queen achieves these effects by following the directions already pointed by Agatha Christie. For example, Van sets up each meeting by sending Martha a scarlet letter that is in the form "Thursday, 4 p.m., A."[26] We learn that Martha has a New York City Guidebook and that twenty-six locations in it are circled in red; each location begins with a dif-

[25] Ellery Queen, *The Scarlet Letters*, New American Library, New York, 1973 (1953), p. 44.
[26] *Ibid.*, p. 37.

ferent letter of the alphabet. These code letters serve also as chapter headings to indicate the course of the action. Hence, like *The A.B.C. Murders*, the book follows its own alphabetic progression. Here the letters structure both the action and the book. Every element of the novel cries out that the work is fictional; each fictional device is turned around to prove that it is real. In the transcendent reality of the fiction, the fictional becomes real; and then we are reminded that the real is itself fictional. This self-reflection is fantastic.

By his own admission, Ellery Queen is a detective in the great tradition:

> "I work on two kinds of cases: those that interest me for their technical difficulty, or those that arouse my indignation. . . . The case I'm currently investigating . . . is a peculiar combination of both. . . . the technical feature of the case consists in the fact that I'm trying, not to solve a crime, but to prevent one."[27]

The escape of the puzzle and the escape of justice. However, despite Queen's assertion, whether made as hero or as author, this work offers only the escape of the puzzle for the escape of justice is abandoned completely. As in *The A.B.C. Murders*, we reach a point in this novel when every character agrees that the culprit has been identified. Queen, however, wants to know the why of it, and his inquiry leads suddenly to a new and deeper meaning of the puzzle. He realizes that Martha is still in danger and races to her rescue. Ellery Queen arrives just in time to see Martha Lawrence shot.

By a medical miracle, no fault of Queen's, Martha lives and is able to attend the trial of her would-be murderer. However, her survival represents no distribution of justice

[27] *Ibid.*, p. 113.

by the great detective; it is a fluke. Granted this fluke, the great detective is not needed to convict the killer: the court has Martha's eyewitness testimony. The book and the reader need the great detective for one thing and one thing only: to tell us *why* the murderer did it, to solve the puzzle. Familiarity with a genre's conventions helps create a readership that forces a genre to explore its own rules. As those rules are reworked and reversed, the genre becomes more fantastic. In the case of detective fiction, the increased use of the fantastic led, through minute stages, to the abandonment of half of the classic consolations of the genre.

In the Nero Wolfe tales of Rex Stout, this abandonment of the escape of justice is carried further still: injustice is allowed to prevail. *Death of a Doxy* (1966) opens with Archie Goodwin, Nero's eye- and leg-man, taking note of the details of the room in which he finds himself with a corpse. The corpse is that of Isabel Kerr, a kept woman engaged to marry Orrie Cather, a sometime agent for Wolfe and therefore a colleague of Goodwin. The police clap Cather in jail "on suspicion," and he calls Archie for help. He and Wolfe confer and decide that Cather is probably innocent. Therefore, they must find the real killer in order to free their fellow.

Interestingly, Wolfe and Company discover the identity of the real killer when the book is only about half over. In the process of the investigation, they have also learned who was keeping Miss Kerr, and have been offered $50,000 by him to guard his anonymity against the publicity of a possible murder trial. The puzzle then becomes not how to spring Cather, but how to spring him without getting the rent-payer's name exposed. Wolfe, of course, does it, but in so doing he extends the time the killer is on the loose and creates enormous tension between the killer and his wife. This leads to the killer's own murder at the hands of his

167

wife and the wife's inevitable apprehension and conviction. As the obligatory uninspired Inspector says to Wolfe:

"Do you realize that if [Cather] hadn't buttoned his lip, if he had told us what he told you, all of it, he would have been out before now, and [the killer] would be in and still alive? Sure you realize it. But *you* had to do it. You had to show once more how sharp you are."[28]

And Wolfe had to earn the $50,000, a fact which, by definition, he can't throw back in the Inspector's face. But we know it, and that seems a sufficient justification for Wolfe's actions in terms of the narrative, for the book ends on the next page with no apologies. With this novel, we see that the justice-escape balance has been shifted so far that the great detective can preside over a world in which puzzles are still solved and yet those solutions result in the distribution of *in*justice.

Rex Stout has made no secret of the conscious way in which he has used Sherlock Holmes and Dr. Watson as models (sometimes inverted) for Wolfe and Goodwin. D. F. Rauber has compared the two detectives against the backdrops of their respective times. In the active Holmes, who places his faith in determinism, Rauber sees the hero of a Newtonian, classical mechanics universe; in the contemplative, action-at-a-distance Wolfe, Rauber, sees the hero of a probabilistic, quantum mechanics universe. He fleshes out this suggestive notion with some extreme observations: ". . . the relation between Archie and Wolfe is almost exactly like that between the experimentalist . . . and the theoretical physicist."[29]

[28] Rex Stout, *Death of a Doxy*, Bantam, New York, 1972 (1966), p. 153.
[29] D. F. Rauber, "Sherlock Holmes and Nero Wolfe: The Role of the 'Great Detective' in Intellectual History," *Journal of Popular Culture*, vol. vi, no. 3, p. 491.

Without doubting that physics, as well as generic conventions, somehow reflects worldviews, and that worldviews are historically changeable, it seems that our attention to the uses of the fantastic offers more convincing and more profitable comparisons than this recourse to simplistic formulations of science. Holmes, in the age of Victorian optimism that held rigid and interwoven views of history, science, and religion, was a man of parts who, believing in science, kept history on track and distributed divine justice. Wolfe, in a fragmented, post-bomb world, is a man in parts who, freed by the history of his genre from distributing justice, solves puzzles for profit, even if injustice is the result. One need not exclude the parallels to physics, which Rauber claims control the development of this popular genre; but one must put those parallels in context. The detective tale has an independent history of its own that reflects the development of a genre under repeated scrutiny by its audience. As that audience requires more of the fantastic, the genre shifts the justice-puzzle balance until something resembling a new genre emerges. That this development is paralleled in physics, where the application of statistics demands closer and closer scrutiny of sub-atomic phenomena, merely confirms the assumption that worldview is a useful concept. But in studying worldview, and in studying the historical development of a genre, attention to the use of the fantastic is the more fundamental analytic tool.

The wide mass audience for "popular culture" reads books less frequently than does the more educated audience for "high art." If conventions must reflect on themselves and develop new uses of the fantastic to accommodate the needs of a mass audience, we would expect that a similar phenomenon would occur more rapidly and more extremely in examples of a given genre intended for a more educated audience. We can see that this is indeed the case by examining the detective fictions of Jorge Luis Borges and Alain Robbe-Grillet.

By 1950, Borges had already published the stories on which his North American fame rests. "The Garden of the Forking Paths" first appeared in English in 1948—in *Ellery Queen's Mystery Magazine*. This story is more thoroughly self-reflexive even than *The Scarlet Letters*; Borges is a writer of Fantasy. The two main characters are Dr. Yu Tsun and Dr. Stephen Albert. Yu is a secret agent for the Germans during World War I. He discovers that Captain Richard Madden has already killed his co-conspirator, and concludes that the inexorable Madden is hot on his own trail. Yu knows that he will not be able to send his vital message to his superiors and so he chooses a surprising tactic: he turns to the phone book, picks out the name "of the only person capable of transmitting the message,"[30] and goes to him. The man is Dr. Stephen Albert, sinologist.

Albert, it turns out, is an expert on Ts'ui Pên. Ts'ui, the reader learns, is special in three ways: first, he is an ancestor of Yu; second, he is remembered by history for having constructed an inescapable—and undiscovered—labyrinth; third, Ts'ui himself disappeared from the earth without a trace. Yu and Stephen Albert have not previously met, but on learning of their common interest in Ts'ui, Albert immediately invites Yu to his home. The directions to the house include passage from the railway station through labyrinthine streets, "but you won't get lost if you take this road to the left and at every crossroads turn again to your left."[31] Similarly, arriving at the house, Yu must thread his way through a garden labyrinth.

[30] Jorge Luis Borges, "The Garden of the Forking Paths," Donald A. Yates, transl., in *Labyrinths*, Donald A. Yates and James E. Irby, eds., New Directions, New York, 1964, p. 21.
[31] *Ibid.*, p. 22.

Yu and Albert meet and discuss Ts'ui's labyrinth, which Albert claims to own. At first it appears to be an ornately inlaid writing desk with secret compartments and slides; but Albert reveals that within the desk he has found a manuscript by Ts'ui, and it is the world of that narrative that is the real labyrinth.

"An ivory labyrinth . . . A minimum labyrinth."
"A labyrinth of symbols," [Albert] corrected.
"An invisible labyrinth of time . . . Ts'ui Pên must have said once: *I am withdrawing to write a book.* And at another time: *I am withdrawing to construct a labyrinth.* Every one imagined two works; to no one did it occur that the book and the maze were one and the same thing. . . . In all fictional works, each time a man is confronted with several alternatives, he chooses one and eliminates the others; in the fiction of Ts'ui Pên, he chooses—simultaneously—all of them. *He creates,* in this way, diverse futures, diverse times which themselves also proliferate and fork."[32]

Stephen Albert's home has a garden of forking paths, forking the way men's choices fork. The garden is also the name of Ts'ui's fiction, and it is the name of Borges' fiction: " '*The Garden of the Forking Paths,*' " [Albert explains] " 'is an enormous riddle, or parable, whose theme is time; this recondite cause prohibits its mention.' "[33] If the title refers to Ts'ui's labyrinthine fiction, then the "mention" may be prohibited in the fictional world, but clearly not in the

---

[32] *Ibid.,* pp. 25-26. There is a growing body of fiction that enacts these complex structural ideas. One of the most delightful is Flann O'Brien, *At Swim-two-birds*, Viking, New York, 1968 (1951), a story with alternate beginnings and endings that includes such events as the birth of a child fathered by an author's character on the author's maid.

[33] Borges, *Labyrinths*, p. 27.

world outside the fiction inhabited by Dr. Albert, who has just mentioned it. The world outside fiction, however, is usually what we think of as the real world; yet here, the real world is fictional. Subliminally, this seems to imply that the fictional world can be real, and Borges, by these fantastic reversals, has created that transcendent reality that gives his literary phenomena meaning.

We may also approach this title from another direction. If Borges' own fiction is indicated by Albert, then the so-called prohibition is clearly not working. This means that the characters are not correctly explaining the operation of the fiction. And yet, the plot of the fiction will indeed show that their explanations are correct, and the reader is thus really trapped in a labyrinth of fictional symbols. The ending of the story turns this labyrinth in on itself when Yu murders his host.

> The rest is unreal, insignificant. Madden broke in, arrested me. I have been condemned to the gallows. I have won out abominably; I have communicated to Berlin the secret name of the city they must attack. They bombed it yesterday; I read it in the same papers that offered to England the mystery of the learned Sinologist Stephen Albert who was murdered by a stranger, one Yu Tsun. The Chief had deciphered this mystery. He knew my problem was to indicate (through the uproar of war) the city called Albert, and that I had found no other means to do so than to kill a man of that name. He does not know (no one can know) my innumerable contrition and weariness.[34]

By becoming a friend, Yu becomes a murderer; by acting randomly, he acts purposefully; by a free press, England

[34] *Ibid.*, p. 29.

relays a secret message; by trapping Yu, Madden helps him complete his mission. Here is a thoroughly self-reflexive detective story: the puzzle is solved because all the rules of puzzle solving are turned inside out, while deterministic rules (turn left and left again) have no bearing on the outcome. It is fate alone that allies Albert's name and interests so well with Yu's ancestry and goals. And yet, mission accomplished, the Germans lose the war anyway. Borges' fiction, which contains the story of the impossible labyrinth of Ts'ui Pên, *is* the impossible labyrinth of Ts'ui Pên, for in it his descendant Yu Tsun, in the Garden of Forking Paths, impossibly chooses all paths simultaneously. Borges has set himself as artist, and Yu as character, an impossible puzzle, and solved it by resort to the fantastic. But in so doing, justice has been abandoned and injustice flourishes: the solver of the puzzle is himself an agent of evil, and his solution brings random death to the scholar and those in his bombed namesake city. It is fitting that the Germans do not profit by this success. Yet, if this failure constitutes justice, it is a justice as fated and beyond human control as the correspondence between Albert and Yu. By continually reversing the ground rules of the narrative world of detective fiction, Borges has created an impossible detective fiction that stands as a direct assault on the assumptions that make detective fiction possible. The very form assaulting itself is the final self-reflexive reversal in Borges' Fantasy.

In comparing the fictions of Borges with those of Chesterton, whom he admired, Robert Gillespie finds many similarities: "Chesterton and Borges both play with similar notions of contradiction, necessity, circular time, and transcendental reality."[35] However, Gillespie finds one signal

[35] Robert Gillespie, "Detections: Borges and Father Brown," *Novel*, Spring 1974, p. 230.

difference: "One major feature Borges drops is the mystery's obsession with justice."[36] If our analysis of "The Garden of the Forking Paths" is correct, then Gillespie is mistaken. For the more intellectual "high art" audience, for Borges and for Yu Tsun, even the self-reflexive complexity of a work like *The Scarlet Letters* was not sufficiently fantastic to prevent the anguished recognition that detective fiction, after all, is too easy an escape. For the more demanding reader who sees further into the conventions of the genre, the genre must become more fantastic to achieve its same affect, to realize an apparently controllable world, where justice can be wrought. After all, Swift's solution to the Irish Question does not seem so fantastic to a reader raised in a world that has witnessed Hitler's solution to the Jewish Problem. By losing the reader and himself in study of Ts'ui's labyrinth, Borges almost makes us forget, as Yu nearly does, the anguishing truth that justice is not in the giving of some great detective. In the penultimate line of the story, Yu explains that he has found the unique solution to the puzzle. But then Yu ends his memoir by realizing that no one can know his "innumerable contrition." This is another fantastic reversal, for *we* realize Yu's contrition. The memoir's final assertion of contrition, with which the story ends, shows that Borges is "obsessed" with justice. It is an overpowering sense of the failure even of correct solutions to distribute justice that leads Borges, Yu, and the reader to a contrition that recalls the perspective that initially drives men to the consolations of detective fiction. In Borges' only story with a Great Detective character ("Death and the Compass"), the detective's *correct* solution to the fantastic puzzle leads him into the trap whereby the arch-criminal can—and does—murder our "hero." In this failure of "justice," we see again the loss of faith that makes

[36] *Ibid.*, p. 226.

readers reject one kind of detective fiction as too simple, but that sends those very readers back to detective fictions that become Fantasy.

Alain Robbe-Grillet writes in this same tradition. *The Erasers* (1953) is the tale of a detective, Wallas, sent to investigate a murder in a provincial capital. His mode of investigation gives the lie to the fundamental mechanism that underlies Holmesian detection. Wallas stumbles into a stationer's shop he intuits is run by the victim's ex-wife; he goes down a street randomly, only to find himself suddenly at the scene of the crime. Perhaps because someone else in the city looks like him, perhaps because the whole world has lost its proper time sense, people report seeing Wallas the day before he arrives. On the day he is in the city, he unwittingly visits just those places he has been reported to have visited. The climax of the investigation occurs when Wallas has somehow decided that the murderer will revisit the scene of the crime. We readers, however, know that the "victim" has never been murdered: he either faked his death with the help of an accomplice or the assassin somehow missed his shot. In either case, the "victim" wishes to let people believe he has been murdered. He surreptitiously returns to his home to retrieve some papers he wants to take with him into seclusion. Wallas, seeing the victim prowling about the house, takes him for the assassin and, in precisely matching detail, kills him as the real assassin was originally to have killed the victim. The detective becomes murderer; the supposed assassin becomes false victim becomes real victim. What makes this tale a Fantasy, rather than a bizarre conflation of mass hysteria and deception, is that the details of the two shootings, in fact all details from the day of the supposed murder to the day of the actual murder, match in *exact geometric detail*. This is coincidence stretched beyond belief into the anti-expected. By

175

relying on the actualization of the anti-expected, Robbe-Grillet, like Borges, makes, within the confines of detective fiction, Fantasy.

Like Borges, Robbe-Grillet's Fantasy reflects both an awareness that life is more unjust than just, and the fond wish that it weren't so. Responding to this sad knowledge, Robbe-Grillet elaborates a style dependent on apparently objective description, and he constructs incidents that appear to follow no mechanistic causation. In so doing, Robbe-Grillet seeks to create a reading experience that is real in itself; its reality is made palpable to the reader by the very excesses of description and narrative confusion. These obtrusively literary techniques prevent the reader from suspending disbelief in the reality of the narrative world that is merely the subject of that reading experience. An example will clarify this.

Madame Bax lives in an apartment with a window that faces the garden gate of the murder house. Wallas goes to inquire of Madame Bax if she may have seen anything suspicious.

"Last night, a man in a raincoat . . ." . . . and to give more weight to her testimony she added that at least one other person had seen the malefactor: before the latter had reached the parkway a man who was obviously drunk came out of the little café—about twenty yards to the left—and took the same direction, staggering slightly; he was singing or talking to himself in a loud voice. The malefactor turned around and the drunk man shouted something to him, trying to walk faster to catch up with him; but the other man, without paying any more attention to him, went on his way toward the harbor.[37]

[37] Alain Robbe-Grillet, *The Erasers*, Richard Howard, transl., Grove Press, New York, 1968 (1953), pp. 108-09.

Wallas himself has by chance taken a room in the little café. One-hundred-twenty pages later he is sitting at the bar trying to ponder the case, but the room is made noisy by a drunk who keeps shouting out versions of a repeating riddle:

> "What animal is parricide in the morning, incestuous at noon, and blind at night? . . . And limps in the morning. . . ."

Wallas leaves. More than any specific task to be accomplished, it is the man with the riddles who is chasing him out of the little café.

> He prefers to walk, despite the cold and the night, despite his fatigue. He tries to organize the various elements he has been able to pick up here and there during the course of the day. Passing in front of the garden fence, he glances up at the house, now empty. On the other side of the street, Madame Bax's window is lit.
> "Hey! Aren't you waiting for me? Hey! Buddy!"
> It is the drunk who is pursuing him.
> "Hey! You there. Hey!"
> Wallas walks faster.
> "Wait a minute! Hey!"
> The jubilant voice gradually fades.
> "Hey there, don't be in such a hurry. . . . Hey! . . . Not so fast. . . . Hey! Hey! . . . Hey! . . ."[38]

Suddenly we see Wallas in the detailed position of "the malefactor." The name Wallas, after all, does not identify a physical human being, but rather locates an element in a total verbal construct, a fiction. We are used to granting such constructs the status of reality by suspending our disbelief in them, but by repeating the context of the malefactor for the detective Wallas, Robbe-Grillet implies that, on two successive days, one "element" *is* the other. This seems

[38] *Ibid.*, pp. 226-27.

fantastic, and seems to deny the conventions of fictional construction by which narrative worlds are realized. *The Erasers* is a new kind of novel, and serves as a convenient paradigm for a whole movement in French literature called the New Novel.

In this New Novel, we do find an underlying explanation, but hardly of a sort that would please Sherlock Holmes. The drunk has posed a version of the riddle of the Sphinx, the riddle that Oedipus solves to become king of Thebes. In a post-Freudian world there are few who will not grant the wide-spread emotional significance attached to the Oedipus myth. Robbe-Grillet pervasively alludes to this myth throughout *The Erasers*:[39] for example, Wallas is sexually attracted to the victim's ex-wife; in the supposed assassin's view, some river flotsam takes on the shape of the Sphinx; Wallas is unaccountably seeking a brand of eraser, the name of which he cannot remember except for the middle letters "di"; and, of course, Wallas becomes the murderer of the man whose murderer he intends to bring to justice. All the facts of the novel fit together perfectly if the narrative world is controlled by a myth; but a world controlled by a myth is a direct reversal of a world controlled by the rational application of knowledge by a great detective serving justice. There is nothing just in Wallas' fate; unlike Oedipus, he hasn't even committed an earlier crime —unless, fantastically, he *is* the would-be assassin.

Oedipus' confusion arose because he thought the oracle's warnings about his parents applied to the people who had raised him. These people, unbeknownst to Oedipus, were not his biological parents. Robbe-Grillet helps add a new dimension to the post-Freudian Oedipus myth by making

---

[39] See Ben F. Stolzfus, *Alain Robbe-Grillet and the New French Novel*, chapter 4, "*The Gum Erasers*: Oedipus the Detective," Southern Illinois University Press, Carbondale, 1964.

us realize that Oedipus' downfall was a result of too easily assuming that *words* referred to known *things*. This same assumption is what, according to Robbe-Grillet, stifles the traditional novel. His writing makes us question this assumption by reversing its consequences. To vitalize the novel, then, and in particular the genre of detective fiction, Robbe-Grillet writes Fantasy. If Wallas had uncovered the right eraser, had realized the Oedipal nature of his problems, they might have vanished; at least, that is the consequence predicted by the theory of Freudian psychoanalysis. However, although we readers may recognize the mythic key to this novel (none did, apparently, until Samuel Beckett pointed out that "di" might refer to Oe*di*pus), Wallas remains caught in a cycle of words and his own fated guilt. The book ends with the text tailspinning into apparently endless, self-reflexive repetition.

The New Novel, developing out of detective fiction, is detective fiction no longer. Robbe-Grillet's escape into Fantasy brought certain qualities of style and temporal manipulation to the fore and these qualities characterize what can only be thought of as a genre apart. Although classic detective stories continue to be written, throughout its history the genre has spawned a series of modifications. In their most extreme forms, these modifications have produced a whole new genre.

One must note that the New Novel also has roots outside of detective fiction. Much modern experimental fiction is based on a widely felt need, regardless of genre, to create narrative worlds that depend on an increase in the use of the fantastic. In Cortázar's "Bestiary," a tiger, seemingly an objective correlative for a woman's sexual fears of her brother-in-law, actually eats the man; in Barthelme's "The Piano Player," the piano, which the wife says frightens her ineffectual husband, actually "strikes him dead"; in Kawa-

179

bata's "One Arm," an impotent old man is enabled to indulge his futile sexual aestheticism when a prostitute, without the slightest gore, gives him her arm for the night; Peter Bichsel constructs a narrative that makes it absolutely plausible that, at this moment, "There is No Such Place as America."[40] We can see the antecedents of this worldwide movement toward the fantastic in the man/cockroach reversal of Kafka; we can see Kafka's roots in Tristram Shandy's father, who both winds his clock and services his wife on the first Sunday of the month; we can see Sterne's roots in the magically opening world of Renaissance exploration that spawned *The Tempest*. And though we can see Prospero as merely another in a long line of figures reaching back through Prometheus to man's first attempt at anthropomorphically dealing with his existential terrors,[41] Prospero is nonetheless a very special figure in that historical line: he is the father of Sherlock Holmes and Nero Wolfe, and it is his bastard progeny who suffer outrageous fate in the New Novel and modern experimental literature.

Prospero ruled the Bermoothes with magic when he was separated from the civilized world of Milan; small wonder that modern writers, when no longer able to civilize narrative worlds by the invocation of the conventions of detective fiction, or of psychological realism, or of Wellsian science

---

[40] Julio Cortázar, "Bestiary," in *Blow-up and Other Stories*, Paul Blackburn, transl., Collier, New York, 1971 (1963); Donald Barthelme, "The Piano Player," in *Come Back, Dr. Caligari*, Doubleday, New York, 1965; Yasunari Kawabata, "One Arm," in *The House of the Sleeping Beauties and Other Stories*, Edward G. Seidensticker, transl., Ballantine, New York, 1969; Peter Bichsel, "There is No Such Place as America," in *There is No Such Place as America*, Michael Hamburger, transl., Seymour Lawrence/Delacorte, New York, 1970 (1969).

[41] For the parallel development of verbal and psychic forms, see Ernst Cassirer, *Language and Myth*, Susanne K. Langer, transl., Dover, New York, 1953 (1946).

fiction, or of any of a host of other genres that still thrive for the mass audience, small wonder that these writers question those conventions, reverse them, make the symbolic the literal, and embark on Fantasy. We can see, by focusing on those elements of detective fictions that are fantastic, how the genre has developed over a 150-year period; we can see too how, in the precarious world of the bomb, Fantasy has moved out of the Victorian nursery and into the adult library. These parallel movements mutually affected each other. Our literary history is much more complex than a mere ordered series of reflexes to cultural needs.[42] Genres in part serve cultural needs by providing escapes from prevailing perspectives and in part create new needs by inventing new escapes to replace those that have worn out.

Prospero found it possible to renounce magic and return to Milan. Today, though some people try to renounce uncertainty and seek a single principle to order their worlds—the Red menace, godlessness, the New Morality, love—those who fully succeed in these efforts are comparatively few. The world will not tolerate great numbers of the inflexible or the fanatic. Those who read Borges and Robbe-Grillet and Vonnegut for escape sometimes realize that there is no longer a believable Milan, else why would they be reading Borges and Robbe-Grillet and Vonnegut? Yet they cannot retreat into fanaticism, and so they suspend their disbelief and return to the Bermoothes: through it all, Agatha Christie sells nearly half a billion books.

What we have been examining is the complex process whereby the intra-literary history of genres, and the extra-

[42] One can, of course, gain much useful insight nonetheless by studying the ways in which literature is responsive to cultural changes. A particularly suggestive work is Roland Barthes, *Writing Degree Zero*, Annette Lavers and Colin Smith, transls., Hill and Wang, New York, 1968 (1953), which manages to use as its main example the whole history of the French novel.

literary history of readers, together generate new genres and modify the perspectives held in the world by readers. This dialectic process, with its concentration on the fantastic, complements normal literary history, which traditionally makes literature a reflex of historic moments or sees literature pursuing an independent growth tied only to the biographies of its authors.[43] Our more detailed analytic methods flesh out traditional insights and join them in a dialectic, developmental view of the history of literature and its audience. Such methods may be applied more widely than to single genres. We have already turned our attention from detective fiction to the worldwide movement for an increase in the fantastic in "high art." We could equally well apply the methods discussed in this chapter to any literary movement.

Gothicism is a literary movement that helped create the climate for the emergence in the nineteenth century of modern science fiction, the thriller, detective fiction, and the psychological novel. This whole movement, like a genre, emerged out of a confluence of earlier literary types and spawned a series of new genres even at the same time that the mainstream of the movement continued and developed on its own. This history, as it emerged in prose narratives, has been well documented by Devendra P. Varma in *The Gothic Flame* (1957). The first and paradigmatic work in this movement was Horace Walpole's *The Castle of Otranto, A Gothic Story* (1764). Walpole claimed that the work

was an attempt to blend the two kinds of Romance, the ancient and the modern. In the former, all was imagination and improbability: in the latter, nature is al-

---

[43] A good description of the ontological problems that confront literary history as an enterprise can be found in the first two chapters of Wesley Morris, *Toward A New Historicism*, Princeton University Press, Princeton, New Jersey, 1972.

ways intended to be, and sometimes has been, copied with success.[44]

Walpole explains that he means Oriental tales (see *The Arabian Nights* or Addison's 1711 sultan story in Spectator #94) to be the ancient and Shakespeare to be the modern. He adduces specifically the psychological truth behind the ghost on the ramparts of Hamlet's castle and thus exposes Otranto's roots at least for the preceding hundred years. But the movement made a splash, and got a name, with the publication of Walpole's "Gothic Story."

The very meaning of "Gothic" historically underwent a transformation akin to the reversal we have seen in detective fiction from the distribution of justice to the distribution of injustice. In the early 18th century, "Gothic" implied barbarous, medieval, and superstitious.[45] We must remember that religious questions still dominated English public thought; universities were closed to Roman Catholics; public office was the preserve of the Establishment. Yet all over England were found examples of indigenous architecture, abbeys, cathedrals, even cottages, that, while reminding everyone of the *Popish* era, nonetheless served as visible artifacts of the *English* heritage. Walpole was an antiquarian and he legitimized the taste for antiquity by joining his own family repute (son of the first Prime Minister), and the fashion for "sentiment," with an interest in "English" architecture. In 1762, Hurd wrote in his *Letters on Chivalry and Romance*, "May there not be something in the Gothic Romance peculiarly suited to the views of a genius and to the ends of poetry?"[46] He had in mind the "Graveyard Poets" like Blair, Young, and Gray, but he reflected a mood

[44] Horace Walpole, *The Castle of Otranto*, Rinehart Press, San Francisco, 1963 (1764), p. 9.
[45] Devendra P. Varma, *The Gothic Flame*, A. Barker, London, 1957 (Russell & Russell, New York, 1966), p. 12.
[46] Quoted *ibid.*, p. 25.

that allowed for the coming Italian (Roman Catholic) thriller that was *The Castle of Otranto*. By this book, and by his own fantastic home at Strawberry Hill, and by his great fame as arbiter of taste, Walpole

> reversed the popular conception of the word 'Gothic'. He changed it from an adjective of opprobrium to an epithet of praise . . . trope for all those spiritual, moral, and cultural values contained for the eighteenth century in the single word 'enlightenment'. . . . but to an average reader the outstanding feature of these tales was not the Gothic setting but the supernatural incidents. . . . The term lost all connotation of 'medieval' . . . and 'Gothic' identified itself with ghastly . . . thus the third meaning 'supernatural' grew out of 'gothic' as a by-product of 'barbarous' and 'medieval'.[47]

Considering only the landmark works, we can see this movement develop. As late as 1786 we see mainstream Gothic rehybridized by Oriental tales[48]—in *Vathek*, Beckford provides not so much palaces as opulent tents and his famous Palace of the Subterranean Fires. It is with *The Monk* (1795) that Matthew Gregory Lewis firmly establishes the third meaning of "Gothic." Although his monumental work showed that Catholic demons, pursued virgins, and monastic supernaturalism still lived, the emphasis on gore brought Gothicism one step from *Otranto*. The channel bed of the mainstream was established.

In the nineteenth century, this mainstream continued strong, but a literary historian might well want to divide the movement into individual genres. For example, 1819 saw

---

[47] *Ibid.*, pp. 12-13.

[48] A powerful discussion of narrative that includes, *passim*, an examination of the processes by which narrative genres fragment and later recombine in new ways is Robert Scholes and Robert Kellogg, *The Nature of Narrative*, Oxford University Press, New York, 1966.

the publication of J. W. Polidori's *The Vampire*, rife with castles, supernaturalism, and, of course, gore. In this form, mainstream gothicism flows down continuously to the present with such works as Prest's enormously popular *Varney the Vampire* (1847), J. S. LeFanu's "Carmilla" (1872), and the most influential version, Bram Stoker's *Dracula* (1897).[49] One should note that it was only in 1823 that England outlawed the ritual of driving a stake through the heart of a suicide.[50] The modern fascination with this genre is made clear by any glance through a movie guide or a visit to an airport bookstall.

Besides the continuing production of works in the mainstream genres of Gothicism, the movement splintered off other genres. As the "enlightenment" qualities of Gothicism were stressed, a market emerged for naturalized Gothicism. Ann Radcliffe is the most important writer of these books which, like *The Mysteries of Udolpho* (1794), give the reader all the thrill of the supernatural, and then tame the delicious fear at the end by explaining the natural causes of the disturbing phenomena. In the development from *Otranto* to *Udolpho*, we see something like the development from Poe to Doyle: whereas Dupin lets us know that the solution is the only object, Holmes first mystifies us, and only then explains his train of logic. In the case of the movement called Gothicism, this development did not merely alter the constituent genres, it created a whole new genre. *Frankenstein* (1818) is perhaps the best example of naturalized Gothic. Only in the middle of this epistolary novel does the reader discover how the "daemon" was created. It is fitting that Polidori and Mary Shelley were friends and began

[49] An excellent bibliography and filmography of the vampire legend is available in the somewhat historical Raymond T. McNally and Radu Florescu, *In Search of Dracula*, New York Graphic Society, Greenwich, Connecticut, 1972.

[50] *Ibid.*, p. 146.

their most famous works in reponse to a mutual challenge to produce something horrific.[51] While Polidori plumbed folklore for a crypto-sexual monster, Shelley looked to the Faust legend for the prototype of the scientist who learns too much. The daemon is the narrative symbol of Victor Frankenstein's knowledge gone beyond control. Such scientific, naturalized Gothicism comes down to the present, through Hawthorne's scientists like Aylmer, into much of modern science fiction. *The Fly* (1958) is a fine film example of this continuing offspring of Gothicism.

Naturalizing the supernatural, of course, is a direct and fantastic reversal of the ground rules that justify the supernatural. It is, after all, fantastic to believe that our fears are all tameable; indeed, just as fantastic as believing that, like Dracula, we are not susceptible to death. One may well speculate that some part of the audience, sated by the conventions of mainstream Gothicism, required an increased use of the fantastic in order to achieve the same affect, the same delicious escape from a world rapidly succumbing to science. To inject science into the supernatural provides that fantastic reversal, and yet that very reversal avoids the supernatural's repudiation of science. By this process, the new genre of naturalized Gothicism was born, a genre that developed right alongside mainstream Gothicism.

When even naturalized Gothicism, where one could have his thrill and laugh at it too, became insufficient, the whole set of generic conventions was reversed and, in 1818, Jane Austen began yet another generic offshoot of Gothicism, satirized Gothicism. *Northanger Abbey* served as a yet more fantastic manipulation of the ground rules of the narrative world and became the fountainhead of a new and

[51] Mary Shelley herself recounts this in her 1831 Introduction to *Frankenstein*, although she implies that Polidori's novel, which was published in 1819, was actually unfinished.

again parallel stream of Gothicism that flows down to us yet with such stories as Ray Bradbury's "Usher II" (1950) and such film spoofs as Roger Corman's *The Little Shop of Horrors* (1960).

In the history of literature, the splitting off of genres by self-satire is a recurrent phenomenon (*Don Quixote*, for example). This splitting creates new genres that can later reinfluence the mainstream, as *Vathek* brought new Oriental energy to Gothicism. As that process of proliferation and influence occurs, the conventions of the original genre, even the conventions of a whole movement, are tamed. If Gothicism can be both naturalized and satirized and yet survive, surely it represents a capacious literary world. Perhaps that is what we mean when we see an idea, retrospectively, as a movement. Once Gothicism does come to represent a whole world, that world can itself be an object of longing, for a literary world is implicitly a world controlled by an artist. To that extent, every literary world represents a fantastic escape from the contingencies of extra-literary reality. By yet another reversal, the thrilling becomes the comforting, and we have romanticized Gothic. Scott's *Quentin Durward* was published in 1823, just five years after *Northanger Abbey*.

Scott's romanticized Gothic was a significant stimulus for the emergence of medievalism in literature. Morris' epoch of rest carried this stream forward, and in modern bookstores we still find the restfully Gothic escape of Walter M. Miller, Jr.'s romanticized monastic world in *A Canticle for Leibowitz* (1959). From the roots of Shakespeare and the Oriental tale, together with the rise of antiquarian interest and sentiment, English literature begat mainstream Gothicism; mainstream Gothicism, by becoming more fantastic, begat naturalized Gothicism; these two genres, by becoming more fantastic, begat satirized Gothicism; and these three

187

genres, by yet another fantastic reversal, begat romanticized Gothicism. Of course, besides the independent histories of each of these streams, we can find crosscurrents, backward eddies, and hybrid works that straddle genres. But the process of historical development is clear, and is clearly parallel within a whole literary movement to the process of historical development within a single literary genre. Both may be examined in new and fruitful ways by consideration of the way works use the fantastic.

# ᕦ VI ᕤ
## The Scope of the Fantastic

THE WIDE range of the preceding chapters, dealing primarily with narrative materials, suggests that the fantastic may be a basic mode of human knowing. The structure of diametric reversal, which signals the fantastic in narrative, might, in theory, arise just as readily in any mental activity that occurs through time or in any temporally extended perception. In theory at least, our perspectives on science, poetry, politics, theology, or on anything whatever, are as subject to reversal as are our perspectives on the ground rules of a narrative world. If such a diametric and fundamental reversal were to occur while perceiving some member of the class of phenomena that is science, poetry, politics, theology, or whatever, then that reversal should produce the affect we associate with the fantastic.

The fantastic is a special quality that we have seen as the defining quality in the genre of Fantasy. Fantasy has had a broad appeal to people of all ages through all the ages. In addition, Fantasy is a genre not only in narrative, but in drama, poetry, painting, music, and film. Considerations of the fantastic have complemented normal methods of inquiry into both genre criticism and literary history because those considerations are based on an atomic element of reader response, what we have called *perspective*. Perspectives can be compounded into constellations of attitudes, genre definitions, even worldviews. In the preceding chapter, we saw how responses to the uses of the fantastic informed the development of a narrative movement, Gothicism. If the fantastic is indeed a basic mode of human knowing, then we should be able to see related and parallel developments in non-narrative materials. If we can indeed do this, then we will have discovered a legitimate ground for aesthetic and historical comparison of human products that are not created in the same medium.

When Hurd first praised "Gothic Romance" in 1762 as "peculiarly suited to the views of a genius," the first "Gothic Story" had yet to be written. Hurd was concerned more specifically with "the ends of poetry."[1] Any history of English poetry can trace the development of the melancholy, mortuary, sentimental, and finally medieval poetry that paralleled the development of Gothic prose. The details of genre development within this stream are not, of course, precisely the same as those within the stream of prose. But those familiar with this period of English letters are used to seeing the similarity as a real and important one. A comparative bibliography of landmark works will make this parallelism immediately clear:

| poetry | prose |
|---|---|
| *Night Thoughts*, Young (1742-1745) | |
| Ossianic poems, MacPherson (1760-1763) | *The Castle of Otranto*, Walpole (1764) |
| *The Lay of the Last Minstrel*, Scott (1805) | *The Mysteries of Udolpho*, Radcliffe (1794) |
| | *Northanger Abbey*, Austen (1818) |
| | *Quentin Durwood*, Scott (1823) |
| *Idylls of the King*, Tennyson (1842-1885) | |
| *The Defence of Guenevere*, Morris (1858) | |
| | *News From Nowhere*, Morris (1890) |

[1] Quoted in Devendra P. Varma, *The Gothic Flame*, A. Barker, London, 1957 (Russell & Russell, New York, 1966), p. 25.

In the prose, we see the movement we have discussed—Gothicism to naturalized Gothicism to satirized Gothicism to romanticized Gothicism—culminating in a work of Morris that has so accepted the later medieval implications of Gothicism that medievalism itself serves as the vehicle for the metaphor of human harmony, the message of the book. In poetry the movement is again from the most strongly emotional to the romantically nostalgic. Of course, the steps along the way are not identical. For example, the rich vein of early eighteenth-century poetic satire had been diverted by cheapening printing techniques into the more popular prose satires (Fielding, Sterne) that flourished after mid-century. There is no satirizer of Gothic poetry of the stature of Jane Austen. Nonetheless, the general movement reflects again what George Kubler calls "aesthetic fatigue,"[2] the general phenomenon that includes the process we have examined whereby familiarity with the fantastic conventionalizes it and spawns an increase of the fantastic in order to produce a continuing strong affect.

Of particular interest to us is the time lag between modifications in the stream of poetry and those in the stream of prose. There have clearly been times in which arts other than poetry were in the vanguard of change—drama, for instance, in the English Renaissance, or prose fiction today. However, in the neoclassic era, the contemporary prescriptive criticism gave poetry an inherently higher value than prose, and consequently attracted the most literarily ambitious and self-conscious practitioners of verbal art. Prose was for the masses, masses who still needed the education and refinement Addison and Steele had offered and Dr. Bowdler would later protect. Poetry attracted those who fancied themselves possessed of sensitive fancies. For writ-

[2] George Kubler, *The Shape of Time*, Yale University Press, New Haven, Conn., 1970 (1962), pp. 71-77.

ers, this meant the exhibition of ever more fantastic images to "excite" melancholy or, if the need be, horror; for readers, this meant that conventions had to be forever revitalized by invention ("What oft was thought but ne'er so well expressed"), invention that led inexorably to modification of the conventions themselves. We have postulated that the speed of modification by increase of the fantastic, by reversal especially of literary conventions, is a function of the familiarity of the audience. When the audience for poetry is the audience of self-conscious and frequent readers, while the audience for prose is the audience of relaxed and infrequent readers, we would expect changes in poetry to antedate those in prose. That is the case in the literary movement called Gothicism. In the careers of two of the most important Gothic writers, in fact, poetry attracted their talents early in life, prose late. Although today we may see writers beginning as novelists and only later turning to poetry, in the marketplace of Victorian England, the opposite was the more general rule. In their own careers, Scott and Morris each reproduce the explicable lag between the development of poetry and the development of prose. This development is explicable especially by reference to the ways in which works of poetry and works of prose used the fantastic.

This delayed parallel between Gothic poetry and Gothic prose is well known. Although it does corroborate the surmise that the fantastic is a basic mode of human knowing, it leaves untouched the question of non-verbal products of the human mind. This realm can indeed be explored, however, by turning to architecture and landscape architecture. The so-called Gothic Revival, after all, was primarily a movement in architecture. Sir Kenneth Clark has traced this movement with great care.[3] We should glance at it to

[3] Kenneth Clark, *The Gothic Revival*, John Murray, London, 1962 (1928).

see if its progress proceeds as we would have predicted based on our study of verbal art.

England's medieval architecture is called Gothic, or Norman, a local brand of the continental Romanesque. The fact that English Romanesque is called by another name indicates what is perhaps the most important fact of English architectural history: Establishmentarian England, the sword of Protestantism, was littered with an architectural heritage that recalled one city alone, Rome. In their rejection of things Popish, beginning in the sixteenth century, the English were laying the groundwork for devaluing the most permanent buildings they possessed.

In architecture, the diametric reverse of Norman is Palladian, or, in other terms, the opposite of Gothic is Classic. While the Gothic gloried in the arch, the Palladian admired proportion. Palladio had given Italy checkerboard floors and cubicle rooms; Inigo Jones gave these same features to English architecture when he built Queen's House (1633). Although Jones himself preferred Gothic architecture until after his second trip to Italy (1612),[4] he nonetheless established Classic architecture in the seventeenth century as the modern, desired, non-Catholic norm. By the time Wren had finished rebuilding London in the last third of the century, Gothic was both antic and antique, "a certain fantastical and licentious manner of building,"[5] as Evelyn says in his *Account of Architects*. Although Clark maintains that throughout England the designs of cottages and farm buildings continued to flow in the indigenous Gothic stream, the more expensive structures of stone were turned over to self-conscious architects who saw themselves as improving the English landscape by erecting perfectly proportioned temples. Wren thought nothing of violating the Gothic lines of St. Paul's with a far-reaching Classic renovation. Meanwhile,

[4] *Ibid.*, pp. 12-13.      [5] Quoted *ibid.*, p. 15.

in the countryside, Gothic churches, abbeys, and outbuildings quietly fell into picturesque decay.

The taste for decay came from two sources: first, the English love of melancholy (see Cheyne's *The English Malady*, 1733) and the associated revival of interest in Shakespeare, especially such melancholic figures as Hamlet on his battlements; and second, the Italian taste for ruins that followed in the train of devout Palladianism. However, the Italian ruins were all of Classic design and the English could not go that far. For one thing, authentic ruins are cheaper than made-to-order ruins, and England's authentic ruins were Gothic. For another thing, "Any ruin might inspire melancholy, but only a Gothic ruin could inspire the chivalry of a crusader or the pious enthusiasm of a monk."[6] So the English adopted the Italian fashion of ruins, but, despite possible anti-Protestant overtones,[7] chose to stick by their own kind of ruins. Indeed, by 1745, Englishmen were *building* ruins to beautify their estates.[8] Those who could afford it built in stone, while those who could only aspire to antiquity built with canvas. But build they did, and from the first they recognized what a fantastic reversal of the assumptions of architecture was implied in such building: they called these ruins "follies." *Folly*, in the early eighteenth century, shared some of the semantic range of *madness*.

When Freud speaks of "psychic economy" and Jung of the "compensatory function" of dreams and neuroses, both reveal our modern attitude that madness represents a flight directly away from some apprehended reality that the individual finds intolerable. Madness is an interior escape, and to the extent that fantasies are sometimes diametric reversals of perspectives held in the conscious mind, we can see the justice in referring to the fantastic in art and the fantastic in psychology by the same term. The Gothic Revivalists

[6] *Ibid.*, p. 58.     [7] *Ibid.*, p. 106.     [8] *Ibid.*, p. 48.

194

indulged their own folly in follies because they felt a need to escape the metrical strictures of Classic architecture and prescriptive architectural criticism.

When, in 1718, Wren was dismissed from the Board of Works, there was a reaction against the native baroque of Vanbrugh. The leaders of the new school . . . had made the Grand Tour, and returned shocked at the Gothic extravagances of Borromini, charmed by the chaste proportion of Palladio. Left to himself, they thought, Vanbrugh bade fair to debauch English architecture as Bernini had debauched Italian. So for about twenty years English architects bent under the Palladian rule, and it was against this narrow Classicism that the real Gothic revivalists reacted.[9]

That "fantastical" manner of building represented a direct escape from the orthodox perspectives ordained for the apprehension of enclosed space.

In the Middle Ages, of course, Gothic has a whole history of its own. This history is usually broken into three stages: early Gothic (Norman), middle Gothic (Decorated), and late Gothic (Perpendicular). These three stages evolve through the process of aesthetic fatigue. The essence of Gothic, as Henry Adams has pointed out,[10] is the upward reaching of normally earthbound stone and the effort to let in ever greater amounts of light. As stone came to be seen as capable of a given height, new techniques had to be invented to make the stone yet more fantastically defy gravity. In this way, the heavy solidity of early Gothic (like White Tower in the Tower of London) gave way to the apparently flimsy leaps of the flying buttresses in late Gothic (like the nave walls of Salisbury Cathedral).

[9] *Ibid.*, p. 18.
[10] Henry Adams, *Mont-Saint-Michel and Chartres*, Houghton Mifflin, Boston, 1963, 1933 (1905).

Although this normal evolution of increasingly fantastic architectural conventions strongly corroborates our notions of art history, more telling in this argument is the way in which nineteenth-century English architecture took a revolutionary turn and threw off Palladianism in favor of Gothicism. In October, 1834, the Old Palace at Westminster burned down, leaving only the Great Hall. England was without a seat of government. Pugin argued that the new building should be "native" English architecture, while the main school of Classicists insisted that Protestant England could not have a Popish capitol. After years of learned and popular and heated debate, Pugin won. Although Barry was the main architect, Pugin designed all the ornamentation and much of the buttressing.[11] And England became the only Western European nation to build its capitol outside the Classical mold. By a radical change of perspective, by suppressing the concern to escape Popery, English architecture escaped Palladianism. Just as, for Morris, the era that first produced Gothic architecture was the symbol for the best in human life, so Englishmen generally could hardly look on Gothic as "fantastical" when Parliament itself was Gothic.

The fact that even non-verbal products of the human mind can be represented by verbal constructs implies the validity of at least partial comparison of work in one medium to work in another. The Cambridge Camden Society (later the Ecclesiological Society) exemplifies this. This group was the Cambridge offshoot of the Oxford Movement; both groups sought to reverse history and re-create what they thought of as a purer and more English faith. The Camdenians wanted church building, as well as church dogma, to return to a more fervent and indigenous

11 Clark, *The Gothic Revival*, chapters 6 and 7.

state. The theological arguments they waged are complex and of little religious interest today. We should note, however, that there is a strong connection between theology and church architecture. For example, a Roman Catholic service requires a building with a screen, with a raised altar, with a choir; the most streamlined Protestant service, which does not rehearse a hierarchical view of congregation, acolyte, priest, and God, needs only a big room of any shape and a place to talk from. In the Victorian age, in which the normative rule was utilitarianism, the excrescences of Gothic should have been perceived as wasteful. But the energetic students at Cambridge argued an older faith, and through a complex process arrived at a nineteenth-century version of a post-Reformation, pre-Cromwell Protestantism.[12] They eschewed the Popish on the one hand, and therefore rejected early Gothic; they denounced the over-enthusiastic on the other hand, and therefore rejected late Gothic. They decided, on principles originally ecclesiological,[13] that the true English church should be done in middle, Decorated Gothic. The Establishment power of these men was such that for fifty years their rules prevailed. No Victorian architect felt impelled to return, in his age of graceful new materials, to the solid Norman, and none dared employ the Perpendicular. The revolutionary building of Parliament in Gothic buttressed the religious arguments of the Camdenians, and the religious arguments of the Camdenians naturalized the fantastical Gothic.

The fantastic exists only against a background to which it offers a direct reversal. We can see this contrast in architecture at the Great Exhibition of 1851. Many students of Victorian England have pointed to this early world's fair as the paradigm of Victorianism: the Exhibition gathered the

[12] *Ibid.*, chapter 8.     [13] *Ibid.*, p. 156.

newest and the best for the optimistic examination of the historically chosen English. And the emblem for the Exhibition itself was its largest single building, the Crystal Palace.

> Joseph Paxton, the designer . . . used standardized iron girders and glass panes because this method appeared to him the cheapest and fastest way to erect a large, temporary building. From this simple, efficient use of the machine, developed the spare functionalism of the modern machine aesthetic.[14]

Housed in one corner of this mechanical building, by way of contrast, was an exhibition of handwork intended to satisfy the fashionable taste for the Gothic. It was housed in the Medieval Court, an environment designed entirely by Pugin.[15]

Ultimately, of course, through years of mutual association, the normative and the fantastic become reconciled; Gothic is naturalized and Palladianism becomes less severe. Just as the Gothic novel finally slipped off, in part, into the not-at-all frightening *News From Nowhere*, so Gothicism finally slipped away from the Camdenians and reached an accommodation with the Classicists. After about 1880, we begin to find buildings (the Natural History Musuem in London is an example) that combine the proportions of Palladianism with the decorations of Gothicism, and all reworked to accommodate the newer construction methods made possible by cheap steel and brick. Once a new norm is established, the old escape is an escape no longer and new escapes must arise in response to the new norm. After 1880, Gothic architecture lived only in intentionally conservative buildings such as cathedrals. And in the twentieth

---

[14] Herbert L. Sussman, *Victorians and the Machine*, Harvard University Press, Cambridge, Mass., 1968, pp. 76-77.
[15] Clark, *The Gothic Revival*, p. 129.

century, no English cathedral has been built in Gothic at all.

William Morris, "perhaps the most promising . . . child of the Gothic Revival,"[16] was supremely important in creating a public awareness of architecture as an integration of numerous modes of art: building, wood carving, glass staining, tapestry weaving, and so on.[17] Morris, like Pugin, designed a total environment, the famous Morris Room in the Victoria and Albert Museum. There one can see, among his wallpaper designs and furniture and stained windows, cabinet painting of medieval scenes that makes clear Morris' membership in the Pre-Raphaelite Brotherhood. Like the Oxford Movement in theology, the Pre-Raphaelite Brotherhood in art was an attempt by a group of committed young men to reverse history. They wished to restore "Nature" to English painting. In the age whose normative painting included the crowd scenes of Tissot, the portraiture of G. F. Watts, and, above all, the ever more vigorous modernism of Whistler, they chose to elaborate a romanticized medieval style that they saw as recalling the harmonious age before the Renaissance emergence of Raphael. The chief practitioners of this school were John Everett Millais, Ford Madox Brown, William Holman Hunt, Dante Gabriel Rossetti, and Edward Burne-Jones, lifelong friend of William Morris.

Morris himself defined the Pre-Raphaelite school in 1891 at a retrospective exhibition in Birmingham. When Rossetti had first begun exhibiting, his fantastic products were rejected by the critics with venom,[18] but by the time of Mor-

[16] *Ibid.*, p. 223.
[17] Paul Thompson, *The Work of William Morris*, Heinemann, London, 1967, p. 49.
[18] Timothy Hilton, *The Pre-Raphaelites*, Thames and Hudson, London, 1970, is the most readable illustrated history of the movement.

ris' lecture, Burne-Jones had been knighted for his art. In this much later atmosphere of acceptance forty-two years after Rossetti first signed *PRB* to a painting,[19] Morris could explain that their art was really a return to "the Great Gothic art" with its "Love of Nature" and its "epical" and "ornamental" qualities. By "Nature," Morris meant symbolic truth, just as Walpole had meant the symbolic truth of Shakespeare's ghosts when he called Gothic prose true to "Nature"; by "epical," Morris meant that the paintings were decidedly not to be thought of as static but rather as dynamic, crucial moments out of a narrative, moments to be temporally *read* by the viewer; by "ornamental," Morris meant that the whole effect should be such that one would be pleased to have the work hang at home, in church, or in some other architectural environment that was regularly inhabited for reasons other than the viewing of paintings. Further, this school was distinct from the "older organic schools, such as the Greek, by its *romantic* quality . . . rather to be felt than defined."[20]

One can see the epical and ornamental together in Rossetti's marvelous illustrations for Morris' *Defence of Guenevere*, for example, or in Hunt's "The Light of the World" (1853-1856).[21] This painting, perhaps the most widely reproduced of the school, shows Christ, his aureole resplendent, but insufficient to throw back the gloom associated with the forest cottage at the door of which he is knocking. From his lamp held low we know he has been searching for some source of light; from his indulgently disappointed look

[19] Paul Harvey, ed., *The Oxford Companion to English Literature*, Oxford University Press, London, 1967, p. 662.
[20] William Morris, "Address on the Collection of Paintings of the English Pre-Raphaelite School" (delivered at the Birmingham Museum and Art Gallery, 2 October 1891), p. 9.
[21] Hilton, *The Pre-Raphaelites*, p. 90.

and softened fist at the door, we know he has already learned that, once again, he may knock, but the door shall not be opened. Many critics find this painting, and many other Pre-Raphaelite studies, too maudlin to be high art. In the same way, some Victorian critics took MacDonald's faithful allegories as too simple to comprise serious theological work. But the great mass of people responded enthusiastically; even today, MacDonald still circulates in paperback and in helpful collections of excerpts, while Hunt is widely available in both museum galleries and at shops offering religious artifacts.

Perhaps the most striking feature of Pre-Raphaelite painting to modern eyes is the extraordinary brilliance of texture combined with precise attention to detail. Even good color reproductions do not do full justice to such a creation as Millais' "Ophelia" (1851-1852),[22] in which the dress of the drowning girl is a light silk dazzling with minute jewels, interwoven with the buds of the flowers picked in her madness, and sparkling with droplets of the very water that is to take her life. This enchanted sheen creates a fairy tale world that fantastically tames death as children's fairy tales, by symbol manipulation, tame life's cruelties.[23] In painting, as is so often the case in other areas of human effort, this new creation of the fantastic is the result of technical innovation that radically changes the conventions of the genre. The Pre-Raphaelites achieved their special effects by use of the "wet white ground." Although earlier English painting, for various reasons, had been quite somber, the Pre-Raphaelites, following a few earlier painters who strove for more light, reversed this entirely.

[22] *Ibid.*, pp. 76-77.
[23] Max Lüthi, *Once Upon A Time: On the Nature of Fairy Tales*, Lee Chadeayne and Paul Gottwald, transls., Frederick Ungar, New York, 1970, pp. 113-114.

The design would be carefully outlined on the canvas, and over this would be painted—only on the portion to be completed at that sitting—a film of white pigment, worked off with a dry brush, then tapped with the brush to ensure evenness. The design would be visible through this thin film, and the painting would be done over it, necessarily with meticulous care, with the smallest of brushes and at a very slow rate. This technique satisfied a demand for brilliance of colour and minuteness of observation, and for a time assumed the status of an article of faith within the Pre-Raphaelite circle.[24]

Understanding how the Pre-Raphaelites achieved their special effects lends support to the cross-media assertion that

The high finish of [Tennyson's] verse, with its polished imagery and the virtuosity of its vowel music, is the exact counterpart of the high technical finish of contemporary painting, the subjects often akin in popular sentimental appeal.[25]

The fantastic worlds of Gothic fiction were paralleled by the worlds of Gothic poetry, Gothic architecture, Gothic landscaping, Gothic theology, and Gothic painting. Indeed, there was even a movement that might well have been called Gothic politics. Ruskin, the first respected critic to spare any praise for the Pre-Raphaelites, was also the originator of the Guild of St. George, a projected agricultural society, much like the Abbey of Thélème, in which all would work according to their abilities and all would be supported. But when Rabelais wrote, he expressed the ideas

[24] Hilton, *The Pre-Raphaelites*, pp. 56-57.
[25] G. M. Trevelyan, *Illustrated English Social History*, volume 4, Longmans, Green, London, 1952, p. 164.

of his times; when Ruskin wrote, he offered a fantastic escape from his. Morris' original intention had been to found a Protestant monastery, along the lines of the Guild of St. George, and when he left Oxford, it was to answer Rossetti's call to art. This, despite and because of the fact that his father had left him a sizeable income based on his years as a stockbroker. In every field of art, and in theology and politics too, we can see the need to break existing molds. This need expresses itself through the fantastic, thereby creating new possibilities and ultimately changing the molds. It is little wonder that we see an intimate relation among the uses of the fantastic in divers media.

Perhaps the hardest working and most important of the Pre-Raphaelites was not one of the original brotherhood but a follower, Arthur Hughes. His "April Love" (1855-1856)[26] is still widely reproduced. But his drawings have achieved even wider circulation because he was, almost exclusively, the illustrator for the works of George Mac-Donald. The perfect agreement between the pictorial style of Pre-Raphaelitism and the verbal style of a fairy tale is evident not only in the children's books like *Curdie and the Goblin*, but in such adult tales as *The Golden Key*.[27]

Seeing Hughes' work with MacDonald and Burne-Jones' work with Morris (for example, "Briar Rose"), one is prompted to explore the relation of the work of the unsentimental Tenniel to that of the gentle Lewis Carroll. Today, of course, we view Tenniel's drawings as strongly related to his political satire, which they certainly are. But in his own day, other aspects of his work would have been immediately noticeable. Carroll is the most thoroughgoing

[26] Hilton, *The Pre-Raphaelites*, p. 104.
[27] A good sample of these illustrations is available in a collection of MacDonald's stories ranging from the obviously juvenile to the clearly adult called *The Light Princess and Other Tales*, Victor Gollancz, London, 1961.

fantastist of the three Victorian writers who have drawn our closest attention. Just as satire implies a move to the right on the continuum of the fantastic when examining works within a single super-genre, so the use of satire is one of the qualities that makes the *Alice* books Fantasies. Tenniel, of course, creates a fairy tale world, or something even a bit more fantastic than that, with such pictures as those of the Cheshire cat disappearing into his own grin.[28] But Tenniel, like Carroll, goes further. The Pre-Raphaelites, by reversing qualities of lighting, for example, created fantastic pictorial worlds. A glance at Millais' *Sir Isumbras at the Ford* (1857)[29] will remind us of this. A glance at the White Knight in the frontispiece to *Through the Looking Glass*[30] will reveal immediately that Tenniel, by further exaggerating Pre-Raphaelite conventions, was not only creating a fantastic world, but like Carroll, directly satirizing such contemporaries as Millais.

As in fiction, so in painting, we see that a consideration of the uses of the fantastic gives us insights that complement those resulting from normal analytic methods. More important than that, however, since these insights are based on microcontextual structural variation, they can be translated from one medium to another and we can with justice decide, for instance, whether Tenniel is more or less successful than Carroll, although they did not work in the same materials.[31] And perhaps most important, the pervasive util-

---

[28] Lewis Carroll, *Alice's Adventures in Wonderland*, in *The Annotated Alice*, Martin Gardner, ed., World Publishing Company, New York, 1960, pp. 88 and 91.

[29] Hilton, *The Pre-Raphaelites*, pp. 80-81.

[30] Lewis Carroll, *Through the Looking Glass*, in *The Annotated Alice*, p. 166.

[31] In my own estimation, Carroll is the more successful. The conventions of political cartoon satire were clear in Tenniel's day, and he works within them, reversing, exaggerating, and inventing when

ity of the fantastic in approaching so many realms of art strengthens our hypothesis that the fantastic represents a basic mode of human knowing, something much broader than the disciplines of criticism, literary history, or art history alone.

In *The Shape of Time*, George Kubler propounds a theory of formal change within genres. He defines a genre in this study of artifacts as a "form-class."

> Every important work of art can be regarded both as a historical event and as a hard-won solution to some problem. . . . As the solutions accumulate, the problem alters. The chain of solutions nevertheless discloses the problem. . . .
>
> The problem disclosed by any sequence of artifacts may be regarded as its mental form, and the linked solutions as its class of being. The entity composed by the problem and its solutions constitutes a form-class.[32]

Using our materials, the problem of revealing hidden guilt[33] is solved by detective fiction; the historical series of actual detective fictions is a class of being; and the general problem with its linked solutions is the form-class which a literary scholar would call a genre. We have seen how within the normal history of the genre, the solutions change and the problem alters, especially as the balance of puzzle to

---

he can. Carroll takes fore-given conventions, reminds us of them, and reverses them, only to reverse again the results. Tenniel's illustrations work wonderfully with Carroll's text, but would be of decidedly less interest alone; Alice is alive in the very words. Hers is the primary fantastic world.

[32] Kubler, *The Shape of Time*, p. 33.

[33] John G. Cawelti, *The Six-Gun Mystique*, Bowling Green University Popular Press, Bowling Green, Ohio, n.d. ". . . the classical detective story is structured around the rationalistic uncovering of hidden guilt." (p. 13)

justice shifts in the development from Poe to Chesterton; we have seen how a reversal of the conventions can emerge that is sufficiently revolutionary to reverse the problem: Wallas, in *The Erasers*, instead of uncovering hidden guilt, acquires it. The terms that Kubler develops for his "History of Things" are exactly convertible to those supporting our literary inquiries based on the uses of the fantastic.

We have seen that, say, in medieval Gothic architecture or in the classic detective story, we can recognize early and late varieties of the genre. In reference to things, Kubler points out that

> Early solutions (promorphic) are technically simple, energetically inexpensive, expressively clear. Late solutions (neomorphic) are costly, difficult, intricate, recondite, and animated.[34]

Any student of the hypertrophied stylistic experiments of modern fiction can see Kubler's statement as a clear description of the recent history of fiction. More important, Kubler is describing in other words the process of increasing reversal, increasing use of the fantastic, that motivates the developments within a genre.

We have postulated that this process of increasing reversal, as in the branching of Gothic fiction, can create whole new genres (form-classes) that rework entirely the conventions of the earlier genre. Further, we have asserted that such late genres can co-exist with the continuing production of members of the earlier genre. This too is Kubler's position, and he offers a striking confirmation of it. Athenian vase painting had consisted entirely of black figures worked on a red clay background. Within this genre, Kubler asserts, modern students with little previous histori-

[34] Kubler, *The Shape of Time*, pp. 55-56.

cal knowledge, can correctly order promorphic, meso-
morphic, and neomorphic examples.

> About 520-500 B.C. . . . a radical technical change was
> introduced. . . . The relation of figure and ground was
> inverted by the simple device of letting the linear en-
> closures have the color of the pottery ground, while the
> surrounding areas were painted black. This new red-
> figure style allowed painters to describe gesture and
> expression by more copious linear means than before,
> but it destroyed the old harmonious relation of figure
> and ground. . . . The innovation permitted the opening
> of a new series.[35]

Kubler's students, presented with red-figure vases, ordered them just as easily, and correctly, into early, middle,
and late examples as they did the black-figure vases. There
does seem to be an internal order in the development of
genres, an order that we can apprehend. Most strikingly,
there exist about ninety "dimorphic" vases, vases showing
late black-figure scenes on one side and early red-figure
translations of these on the other. It seems clear that at
some crucial moments, artists must choose "between custom
and innovation."[36] In this case, it is apparent that the innovation must have appeared truly fantastic, have offered a
whole new way of seeing, for in the most obvious sense, the
emergence of the new genre, with its new problems and
new solutions, represented a radical, diametric reversal of
the world of conventions that had preceded it.

"Dimorphism" is a much more widespread phenomenon
than one might guess. One may easily find a novel like *The
Jungle*, which is primarily of one type (the pessimistically
naturalistic), suddenly break its own decorum and shift at

[35] *Ibid.*, p. 119.     [36] *Ibid.*

the end to a radically different type (the optimistically socialist utopia). Edmund Carpenter recounts how a filmed version of an initiation rite nearly supplanted the actual rite, the two possibilities existing simultaneously for a while, but the ritual winning out when the film quality got too poor.[37] André Bazin suggests that

> it would be interesting . . . to study, in the illustrated magazines of 1890-1910, the rivalry between photographic reporting and the use of drawings. The latter, in particular, satisfied the baroque need for the dramatic.[38]

Drawings, of course, were neomorphic at this time. Photographs, on the other hand, were promorphic. From the perspective of many painters in the nineteenth century, photography was the diametric opposite of painting. The fantasist Lewis Carroll was one of his century's best and most avid photographers.[39] At key moments in the development of human perspectives, man always confronts a fantastic leap.

Kubler asserts, on the basis of his study of "things," that "Structural forms can be sensed independently of meaning . . . structural elements undergo more or less regular evolutions in time without relation to meaning."[40] Although his book is solid and incisive, on this one point, however central, he seems mistaken. Our study of the fantastic has

[37] Edmund Carpenter, *Oh, What A Blow That Phantom Gave Me!* Holt, Rinehart and Winston, New York, 1972, pp. 134-135.

[38] André Bazin, *What Is Cinema?* University of California Press, Berkeley, 1967, p. 11.

[39] A full account of Carroll's surprisingly great importance as a photographer is available, with a generous sample of illustrations, in Helmut Gernsheim, *Lewis Carroll Photographer*, Max Parrish & Co., London, 1949.

[40] Kubler, *The Shape of Time*, pp. vii-viii.

shown that the "evolution" of style within a genre, and the "revolution" of style into a new genre, is a result of the apprehension, by artist and audience, of the "meaning" of the conventions that define the artistic world. There is an evolution in the nineteenth-century English Gothic, but this evolution can hardly be divorced from the Popish meaning attributed to at least early Gothic; there is an evolution, after World War I, in the detective story, but this evolution can hardly be divorced from the simplistic feelings readers attached to the older Sherlock Holmes. There is an inexorable evolution within and among genres, and Kubler has described this process in a general way that embraces all artifacts and is convertible to considerations of verbal constructs. We have seen that the motive force behind this evolution is precisely the meanings people apprehend from the art and objects around them.

Robert Plank, in discussing cultism, especially the 1950s' rage for flying saucers, argues finally that "the mental process of creating imaginary beings is in essence a duplication of a relationship of crucial emotional significance. . . ."[41] This relationship, for saucer lovers, is the Oedipal one. The archetype of the mad scientist (a human version of the all-powerful Martian) is Prospero, and the ultimate emotional significance of imaginary beings, Plank argues, lies in our urge to have Prospero order our world. We each have within us the soul of a Ferdinand or of a Miranda.

Whether this urge for order need be explained by reference to a monomyth, whether this explanation is so widely useful that it may legitimately relate William Shakespeare and Edgar Cayce, it is still clear that as scientist, as detective, as Shane, or as Superman, the ordering figure often enough presides over narrative worlds that are indeed fan-

[41] Robert Plank, *The Emotional Significance of Imaginary Beings*, Chas. C. Thomas, Springfield, Illinois, 1968, p. 149.

tastic in their regularity, and attract us for that very reason. Even the scientist Faust was tempted by Mephistopheles; we all seek an ultimate knowledge that will allow us to control our worlds. The world being what it is, such control is fantastic.

One realm of activity in which people habitually comfort themselves with the sense of control is games. By games, here, I include also sport, fraternity rushing, medieval jousting, and quiz programs, indeed, any activity that is structured by convention in such a way that people agree to assign known values to allowable actions and in which they can, through these actions, produce a condition that the participants will agree to value. What makes checkers a game is that both players subscribe to certain conventions (rules) and the play by these rules can result in a condition wherein one has "lost" all his "men." This, surprisingly enough, gives the other participant pleasure.

John G. Cawelti, in studying the Western story, argues that Westerns are so highly conventionalized that they can be expressed as "formulas." His formula is discursive, and capacious enough to include numerous variations, but for our purposes we need only note that in a typical Western (say *Shane*), the hero, possessing the wild skills of the outlaws (range riders, Indians, or other inhabitants of the countryside), becomes convinced that he should employ his skills to protect the values of the townspeople (homesteaders, farmers, schoolmarms) who are not able to protect themselves. He does protect them, mediating between the two groups and passing between their two terrains, but his success is a self-abnegation that requires him to return to the wilderness (Natty Bumpo, Shane) or give up gun-fighting and settle down (the Virginian). Cawelti suggests that detective stories, fairy tales, indeed many widespread genres, are essentially "formulas." And formulas, he quite rightly proposes, are, in their mode of knowing, equivalent to games.

> . . . the game dimension of formula is a culture's way of simultaneously entertaining itself and of creating an acceptable pattern of temporary escape from the serious restrictions and limitations of human life.[42]

Put in our terms, games/formulas/fictions create fantastic worlds that allowably offer diametric alternatives to perceived reality.

Games are much more common and much more various than Cawelti suggests, however. There are countless "games people play." In *A Farewell to Arms*, Lt. Henry and Catherine Barkley, both lost in the cruel and chaotic realities of war, silently, conventionally, agree to be in love. Catherine's pathetically ritualistic assertions of love are required to make the game believable. Ultimately, the great effort expended in sustaining this mutual fantasy is seen by the protagonists as heroic and engenders real love. At that crucial point, the original chaos of reality reasserts itself and Catherine dies in childbirth. So much for living in our fantasies. Reality, Hemingway tells us, is not so kind. And yet, we all live in games time and again. We structure our lives, our sense of sexual roles, and our relations with fellow workers by subtle political conventions to which we subscribe because we need the consolation of a tame world. If one can accept the intricacies of a social system as a highly complex analog of a simple game, then one can see that the escape offered by a "formula" shares an essential element of structure with any fantastic escape offered by any mental construct, any complex set of conventions, even, in a fundamental way, with those conventions necessary for a so-called realistic novel.

[42] Cawelti, *The Six-Gun Mystique*, p. 32.

Novels, games, and even love affairs have a certain sense of wholeness about them; so do political campaigns and Greek tragedies. Life, on the other hand, does not. In the great chain of Aristotelian causation, every effect came from a prior cause, every effect in turn is a cause. In our post-Heisenberg world, we recognize that even the minimal act of observing an effect serves as a new cause, and so the chain of cause and effect runs on endlessly.

Events have the fatal weakness, as non-art, of

carrying no necessary or intended significance. As Wallace Stevens observes,

> Twenty men crossing a bridge,
> Into a village,
> Are twenty men crossing twenty bridges,
> Into twenty villages.[43]

But Stevens' poem, though it contains this idea, is itself apprehended as full of significance; it is read as a whole.

Aristotle, in a most famous passage,[44] writes that a tragedy

is an imitation of an action which is complete and whole. . . . "Whole" is that which has beginning, middle, and end. "Beginning" is that which does not necessarily follow on something else, but after it something else naturally is or happens; "end," the other way round, is that which naturally follows on something else, either necessarily or for the most part, but nothing else after it; and "middle" that which naturally follows on something else and something else on it. So, then, well-constructed plots should neither begin nor end at any chance point but follow the guidelines just laid down.

[43] Harold Toliver, *Animate Illusions*, University of Nebraska Press, Lincoln, 1974, p. 101.
[44] Aristotle, *Poetics*, Gerald F. Else, transl., University of Michigan Press, Ann Arbor, 1970 (1967), p. 30.

Life, unlike books, will not subordinate "chance" to "guide-lines"; in life, we are always in the middle. We may think we see the decisive end when someone dies, for example; but the next day, the paper boy still stops at the door of the deceased. Our perception of necessary causation and the paper boy's and that of twenty men crossing a bridge, each perception may be different. Aristotle's definition relies heavily on the idea of "naturally," and by using this term he glorifies a notion of normalcy that might better be called "prevailing worldview." And worldviews, we know, are subject to change.

We began the discussion of the fantastic by discovering it as an affect found abundantly in Fantasy. This affect is generated by a direct reversal of the ground rules of a narrative world. Throughout the history of rhetoric, men have felt the urge to distinguish life and art, to ponder the escapes of art, to seek the consolations of art. It seems reasonable that anyone who has lived beyond the death of a loved one must realize that "life," the endless chain of events, is in fact chaotic and never legitimately divisible into "wholes." And yet, every work of art, every goal-directed task, every game played with another or even with oneself, all of these attempt to impose man's perspectives on an intractable universe. The reality of life is chaos; the fantasy of man is order.

Perhaps no novelist is so unanimously accepted as a "realist" as is Henry James. The Ambassadors[45] begins with the following: "Strether's first question, when he reached the hotel, was about his friend." In this sentence we already sense a voice speaking to us; we sense a purposefulness behind the report. We don't know who Strether is, we don't know his friend, and we don't know which hotel is so important to the overall report that it is "the" hotel. And yet,

[45] Henry James, The Ambassadors, Riverside Press, Cambridge, Mass., 1960 (1903), p. 17.

prompted by the conventions of third person narration,[46] we assume that all of this is significant. Unlike events, this is art. This already functions as part of a whole the reader predicts will emerge. No matter how realistic James' novels may be, they are not real.

In real life, our perspectives act not only to focus our attention but to blind us to irrelevancies. The importance of money, for some people, makes any mention of it prominent. This is a useful sensitivity in a real live capitalist society. On the other hand, as the muckrakers pointed out, the prominence of money diminishes other affects. The owners of the slaughterhouses in Chicago and in Sinclair's *The Jungle* alike seemed not to feel the human misery caused by their attention to financial enrichment. To the extent that one looks at the forest, the trees disappear; and vice versa. In order to deal with the rush of sensory data we might theoretically perceive, we filter that data and sense only those stimuli that we are keyed to sense. Although the exact keying of perspectives varies widely from culture to culture, and varies even among individuals within a culture, the process of keying is itself a universal human phenomenon. And each time someone points out that the obvious was missed, each time our keying is shown up as a necessary, but not absolutely reliable, way of knowing the real world, we realize that a world constructed by convention is in some important way the direct opposite of the real world.

In the real world, we don't notice people who pass us unless we are keyed to them, unless they are recognized or they are abnormal or they call out to us. Without keying,

---

[46] A clear and bold argument that minimal conventional signals such as "he said" are sufficient to indicate fiction is available in Thomas J. Roberts, *When Is Something Fiction?* Southern Illinois University Press, Carbondale, 1972.

events do not take part in wholes for us, and we assume they have no significance; we must assume this to survive. In books, however, we assume the exact opposite. Having no reference for Strether, or his friend, or "the hotel," we assume nonetheless that they will emerge as significant. The world of art, the world of games, the world of politics, so many worlds men make for themselves, are in a very fundamental way fantastic. If the reader and the author can share the conventions whereby the narrative world is constructed, then the fantasy of that world can be indulged; if Catherine and her lieutenant had been left alone by the weaknesses of the flesh and the chaos of war, their love would have been as good as real; perhaps the same as real. But weakness and chaos did not leave them alone. All art, all mental wholes, are, to some extent at least, fantastic.

Returning for a moment to the idea of the continuum of the fantastic, we can now see that at the far left-hand side of the scale, we still find non-zero values. A minimally fantastic work of art, *The Ambassadors* for example, is still somewhat fantastic just because it is a work of art and therefore offers us a safe, controlled world in which caution is unnecessary and where we can afford to suspend disbelief. In the world outside the text, as we have seen, we all function by tacitly accepting[47] a host of perspectives that both blind us and focus our attention. Our division of the world into talking things (people) and non-talking things (rocks and flowers, for example) is one of the ground rules of our real world. Early in *Alice in Wonderland*, despite all

[47] See Michael Polanyi, *The Tacit Dimension*, Doubleday, Garden City, New York, 1966. This concise essay powerfully suggests that what we must assume tacitly (e.g., the workings of language) has a more profound effect than what we consciously examine (e.g., a story) for the sake of which we have made our tacit assumptions. This is a more far-reaching statement of the principle McLuhan rehearses under the rubric, "The medium is the message."

the other odd happenings, we hold to the external ground
rule that flowers don't talk simply because that rule has not
been challenged. When it is reversed, the reversal produces
the affect of the fantastic. Once that reversal occurs, the internal ground rules allow flowers to talk and the fantastic
thing would be to find a mute flower. By claiming our attention for every detail of the narrative world, a James novel
reverses one basic external ground rule. The text then proceeds as unfantastically as possible. Other works begin by
reversing larger numbers of external ground rules in order
to establish their narrative worlds, this constellation of reversals often signalled conventionally ("Once upon a
time. . . ."). Such works are further to the right on the continuum of the fantastic than is *The Ambassadors*. And yet,
within a given genre, or in a given narrative world, the still
operative ground rules imported from the external world,
or even the newly created internal ground rules, can be reversed again. The more of this that occurs, the more fantastic a work is, and the further to the right on the continuum
of the fantastic. By understanding the mental reversal im-
plicit in a realistic novel, we can see the dialectic relations
possible between external and internal ground rules.

The fantastic gives us the chance to try out new, "unreal-
istic" possibilities, and thus, perhaps, change seen reality.
At the end of the last century, George M. Stratton experi-
mented with inverting glasses, lenses that made everything
look upside down.[48] Invariably, his subjects would first feel
disoriented and troubled, then their vision would be merely
confused, and finally everything would seem normal. The
shock of this direct reversal had a real-life affect much like
the controlled affect of the fantastic in art. And just as external ground rules are exchanged for internal ones in art,

[48] Thomas S. Kuhn, *The Structure of Scientific Revolutions*, University of Chicago Press, Chicago, 1970 (1962), p. 112.

so in this real-life experiment, reversal taught Stratton's subjects a new way of seeing.

Fantasy is the genre in art or literature or film or any other medium that makes the consideration of fantastic reversals its very heart. Although most of the materials of our inquiry have been narrative, perhaps the best paradigm for Fantasy is graphic. M. C. Escher[49] calls the following drawing "impossible":

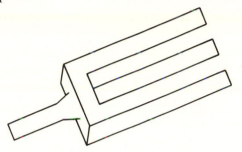

This three-pronged tuning fork cannot exist. On the other hand, neither can speeds faster than light exist, or so we believe. Yet the physical fact is not nearly as disturbing—or fantastic—as the drawing. The physical fact of limits is an inhuman and remote truth we may all accept, but it doesn't affect us. This drawing does. The explanation is simply that this drawing is *about* human perception. If you cover the tips of the prongs with your hand, you will see a schematic representation of a two-pronged tuning fork expressed by the conventions of three-dimensional perspective; if you cover the base of the tuning fork, you will see three rods expressed by the conventions of two-dimensional perspective. By reversing the viewer's perspectives within a single pictorial world, the work becomes fantastic. By insisting, as drawings often seem to, that the aim be representation,

49 M. C. Escher, *The Graphic Work of M. C. Escher*, Macdonald, London, 1967, p. 16.

this "impossible" drawing assaults those external rules we habitually import into the reading of line drawings. A real Fantasy uses the fantastic so essentially and so constantly that one never escapes its grip into the security of a fully tamed world for more than a moment. This drawing, which will only hold still by having one end held down, fulfills this requirement exactly: it is, though utterly non-verbal, a Fantasy.

This drawing is structurally ambiguous: any part of it can legitimately be taken as having either of two meanings, depending on the perspective with which one looks at that part. As Gombrich says, "ambiguity as such cannot be perceived."[50] Hence the evanescence of the perception of this drawing—and the evanescence of *Alice*. To perceive ambiguity is to abandon perspective. But perspective as such, the process of mental keying, has survival value. We will not abandon perspectives entirely. Instead, we can only exchange particular perspectives for alternative ones, usually alternatives that are felt to be diametrical oppositions. Kuhn reports an experiment[51] in which people are shown playing cards occasionally including such anomalies as a black four of hearts. Almost invariably, the subjects failed to notice the anomalies but instead identified the cards blithely as either the four of hearts or the four of spades; the non-anomalous cards were identified correctly. We reject reality in the face of our perspectives. "I wouldn't have seen it if I hadn't believed it." The wonderful, exhilarating, therapeutic value of Fantasy is that it makes one recognize that beliefs, even beliefs about Reality, are arbitrary.

[50] E. H. Gombrich, *Art and Illusion*, Princeton University Press, 1969 (1960), p. 259.
[51] Kuhn, *The Structure of Scientific Revolutions*, pp. 62-63.

Borges writes that "reality is not verbal."[52] He is attempting to distinguish between things as they are and mental constructs. Indeed, he offers stories that might seem to confirm his position. A particularly haunting tale is that of "Emma Zunz," who one night learns of her father's miserable death in a foreign land. She is a virginal, middle-aged factory worker. She entices a foreign sailor from a ship that is about to sail to roughly violate her. Then she methodically calls up her employer and offers to reveal to him the details of an impending strike. While she waits for him to arrive, her thoughts reveal to us her knowledge that the employer had been her father's business partner and had ruined him. The employer does not know Emma's real identity. When he arrives at the office, she kills him. The story ends with the following:

> Then she picked up the telephone and repeated what she would repeat so many times again, with these and with other words: *Something incredible has happened . . . Mr. Loewenthal had me come over on the pretext of the strike . . . He abused me, I killed him . . .*
>
> Actually, the story *was* incredible, but it impressed everyone because substantially it was true. True was Emma Zunz' tone, true was her shame, true was her hate. True also was the outrage she had suffered: only the circumstances were false, the time, and one or two proper names.[53]

"Emma Zunz" does not teach us that reality is not verbal. Instead, it teaches us that reality is not merely what we

[52] Jorge Luis Borges, *Other Inquisitions 1937-1952*, Ruth L. C. Simms, transl., Washington Square Press, New York, 1966, p. 42.
[53] Jorge Luis Borges, "Emma Zunz," Donald A. Yates, transl., in *Labyrinths*, Donald A. Yates and James E. Irby, eds., New Directions, New York, 1964, p. 137.

think it is. This can be seen by analogy in another "impossible" drawing.

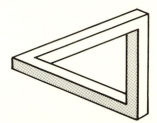

Unlike the tuning fork, the triangle does not employ two conflicting systems of perspective; instead, it pits one orientation of a system of perspective against another orientation of that same system. The result is equally fantastic. If one covers any *one* of the corners, the exposed remainder will be seen as a perfectly good partial representation of a solid three-dimensional form expressed by the conventions of three-dimensional perspective. This is true covering *each* corner. Yet, the same lines are involved in expressing three different forms with three different orientations. The drawing is structurally ambiguous; and it demonstrates that the reversal of internal ground rules can be just as affecting as the reversal from external to internal ground rules. Emma Zunz, in her report to the police, plays with their moral perspectives and ours, and our inability to perceive ambiguity itself makes it impossible to simultaneously see the events of her story in their two proper lights. We sense that evanescence again. Borges' tale, by the nature of its structure and not by the nature of verbal constructs, is fantastic.

In a sense, the impossible triangle is self-reflexive; it comments on its own ground rules. Borges has thought about self-reflection:

> Why does it make us uneasy to know that the map is within the map and the thousand and one nights are

within the book of *A Thousand and One Nights*? Why does it disquiet us to know that Don Quixote is a reader of the *Quixote*, and Hamlet is a spectator of *Hamlet*? . . . those inversions suggest that if the characters in a story can be readers or spectators, then we, their readers or spectators, can be fictitious.[54]

Self-reflection, in raising questions about the ontology of the real world, serves to keep our perspectives "in perspective." The fantastic confusion of the external and internal worlds is the most common device of art, and is found even more frequently in the more highly fantastic art. "If ever you make a book of this,"[55] one character will say to another; Ellery Queen reads his own mystery magazine; Alice doesn't know if she dreams the red king or if he dreams her; we all, in reading books, look at ourselves. Self-reflection is fundamental to human perception.

In the science fiction novel *Solaris*, Stanislaw Lem creates a world that is one large sentient ocean. This ocean somehow can project matter and creates "people" out of the memories of the members of a scientific research team. These creations are essentially projections of the minds that remember.

> "You are not Gibarian."
> "No? Then who am I? A dream?"
> "No, you are only a puppet. But you don't realize that you are."
> "And how do you know what *you* are?"[56]

Borges' question exactly.

In his essay on "The Uncanny," Freud comes to decide

54 Borges, *Other Inquisitions*, p. 48.
55 William Morris, *News From Nowhere*, James Redmond, ed., Routledge & Kegan Paul, London, 1970, p. 72.
56 Stanislaw Lem, *Solaris*, Joanna Kilmartin and Steve Cox, transls., Berkley, New York, 1970 (1961), p. 142.

that: "the uncanny is that class of the frightening which leads back to what is known of old and long familiar."[57] The uncanny, of course, is always fantastic, and, according to Freud's analysis, only arises when it calls up something from one's own depths.

> . . . an uncanny effect is often and easily produced when the distinction between imagination and reality is effaced, as when something that we have hitherto regarded as imaginary appears before us in reality, or when a symbol takes over the full functions of the thing it symbolizes, and so on.[58]

One of Freud's primary examples is "The Sandman," by Hoffmann. In this story, we see clearly how childhood fears, though they arise because the world is indeed a threatening place, nonetheless are projections of one's own mind, important projections that finally drive the protagonist to suicide. We need the uncanny in art, we need all fantastic effects in art, because, as Lem writes, "We need mirrors."[59] In *Solaris*, the ocean fully takes on the function of the mirror it symbolizes.

Vonnegut's fictional science fiction writer, Kilgore Trout,

> called mirrors *leaks*. It amused him to pretend that mirrors were holes between two universes.
>
> If he saw a child near a mirror, he might wag his finger at a child warningly, and say with a great solemnity, "Don't get too near that leak. You wouldn't want to wind up in the other universe, would you?"[60]

[57] Sigmund Freud, "The 'Uncanny,'" in *The Standard Edition of the Complete Psychological Works of Sigmund Freud*, James Strachey, ed., The Hogarth Press, London, 1957 (1919), vol. XVII, p. 220.
[58] *Ibid.*, p. 244.     [59] Lem, *Solaris*, p. 81.
[60] Kurt Vonnegut, Jr., *Breakfast of Champions*, Delta, New York, 1973, p. 19.

There is a truth in calling mirrors leaks. A second view, the mirror that may be the familiar dredged up uncannily, offers us new, fantastic realities. There is a seductive danger in flirting with a second reality. But note that Vonnegut has Trout warn a *child*. Typically, the fantastic is more acceptable in the context of children. It is clear even to adults that at least for children fantastic worlds are useful mirrors. As Lüthi suggests,[61] the fairy tale, by handling cruelty symbolically, implies to the child that there can be a world in which cruelty is tamed. Our mirrors shape our perspectives.

At the end of his book, Lüthi leaves considerations of children to consider readers more broadly. Although

> from the eighteenth century on into the twentieth, the struggle was waged against the miracle . . . one cannot say that literature in the twentieth century is antipathetic toward what is fantastic, fabulous, and miraculous. The miracle, though not accepted as real, has become an image and appears in many forms, even though it may be disguised in the form of the absurd or the incomprehensible.[62]

Indeed, such an absurd play as Ionesco's *Rhinoceros*, in which people become pachyderms under the social influence of a fascist state of mind, strikes us as fantastic, even uncanny, as it dredges up our own herd fears by letting the symbol of rhinoceros take over the full functions of the state of mind it symbolizes. The fantastic, even the enchanted, is common in contemporary literature.

A specific fantastic technique that exemplifies self-reflection and the engrossing of symbolic function is the self-conscious use of *characters* as *people*.[63] In Raymond

[61] Lüthi, *Once Upon A Time.*
[62] *Ibid.,* p. 157.
[63] Here again, Flann O'Brien's *At Swim-two-birds* is a useful example.

223

Queneau's *The Flight of Icarus*, the character Icarus escapes M. Lubert, his author, and goes off into the narrative world. There he meets a good-hearted hooker named LN (not Hélène in this orthographic world) and they fall in love. One day, Icarus is sitting drinking absinthe when LN returns from earning their livelihood.

> LN (coming in)   My pet! that's your howmanieth?
> ICARUS   My seventh.
> LN   But you've only got five saucers.
> ICARUS   I was anticipating. I'm an anticipatory character.[64]

Such self-reflection is not mere games playing. The fantastic has many specific functions, but Queneau's self-reflection underscores the general mirroring function by capitalizing on an insight like Borges' that we might be fictitious. In the following, Icarus is conversing with another escaped character:

> ICARUS   Once we are free, don't we have the same desires, the same needs? The same faculties? Don't we have to obey the same necessities of life?
> MAITRETOUT   Once we're free, yes, but we always run the risk of returning to a different state if we're caught. The other men in the street don't.
> ICARUS   How do we know? It may all come to the same thing. They may be characters of some other sort of author.[65]

This feeling, even in our scientific age, rings uncannily true. And it is the typically fantastic technique of self-reflection that makes this truth palpable.

[64] Raymond Queneau, *The Flight of Icarus*, Barbara Wright, transl., New Directions, New York, 1973 (1968), p. 71.
[65] *Ibid.*, pp. 166-167.

In *Totem and Taboo*, Freud discusses the "omnipotence of thought," the fantasy (in the strictly psychological sense) that one can think things into happening or existing.

If we accept the evolution of man's conceptions of the universe mentioned above, according to which the *animistic* phase is *succeeded* by the *religious*, and this in turn by the *scientific*, we have no difficulty in following the fortunes of the "omnipotence of thought" through all these phases. In the animistic stage man ascribes omnipotence to himself; in the religious he has ceded it to the gods, but without seriously giving it up, for he reserves to himself the right to control the gods by influencing them in some way or other in the interest of his wishes. In the scientific attitude towards life there is no longer any room for man's omnipotence; he has acknowledged his smallness and has submitted to death as to all other natural necessities in a spirit of resignation. Nevertheless, in our reliance upon the power of the human spirit which copes with the laws of reality, there still lives on a fragment of this primitive belief in the omnipotence of thought.[66]

It is this small retained fragment that we dredge up again and again not merely in creating the uncanny, but in creating the fantastic. The tamed world, the controlled world, the world whose ground rules are no longer confining, these are the worlds that help us overcome too much reality. Even such a modern cynic as Shaw bases his popularity on this consolation. The Hell of *Man and Superman* (1903), of course, is merely the projection of the minds of those who inhabit it. So much, Shaw seems to say, for religion. But this

[66] Sigmund Freud, *Totem and Taboo*, in *The Basic Writings of Sigmund Freud*, A. A. Brill, ed., Modern Library, New York, 1938, p. 875.

scientific irony incorporates the notion that men can shape their afterlives by shaping their psychic lives, and in attempting a fantastic debunking of religion, Shaw offers the fantastic consolation of an older animism. If Freud is right and we cherish a fragment of our childish belief in the omnipotence of thought, then the fantastic is vital to a fundamental sector of our psychic lives and Shaw is great, at least in part, because he serves that sector so well.

Writing to a friend about *The Castle of Otranto*, Walpole said that "a god, or at least a ghost, was absolutely necessary to frighten us out of too much sense."[67] There is a dark side to the fantastic, and a light side, the ghost and the god. Walpole chose the dark, but Lewis Carroll did not. Both Freudian dream analysis and Jungian dream analysis are based on (differing) notions of the mechanism by which the unconscious of our minds, which is the diametric opposite of the conscious, creates fantastic narratives that can be decoded to discover our "real" perspectives. This is precisely equivalent to our analysis of Fantasies to determine normative worldview. But in today's psychoanalytic world, some tend to think of unconscious urges only as out-of-control and perhaps base, the fantasies of the ghost. The god lives too.

In the world of English speakers, perhaps the paradigmatic Fantasist is the delightful Lewis Carroll. For speakers of German and French, the paradigmatic Fantasist is the ghastly Hoffmann. The continental words for "fantastic" have a bit of the tone we associate with "macabre." Freud and Jung, German speakers, created the modern reception of the fantastic. But we can choose to look at the daylight instead of the gloom. In English, someone can feel "fantastic!" The fantastic reveals not only our deepest fears, but

[67] Horace Walpole, quoted in Varma, *The Gothic Flame*, p. 55.

also our greatest aspirations; not only our hidden shames, but also our finest hopes. Thomas Kuhn has shown that even in the scientific perception of reality, we establish perspectives (which he calls paradigms), and we make revolutionary scientific progress only by fantastically reversing them.[68] This important use of the fantastic to reshape the world in which we live should not surprise us, for, as Tolkien writes

> creative Fantasy is founded upon the hard recognition that things are so in the world as it appears under the sun; on a recognition of fact, but not a slavery to it.[69]

Fantasy represents a basic mode of human knowing; its polar opposite is Reality. Reality is that collection of perspectives and expectations that we learn in order to survive in the here and now. But the here and now becomes tomorrow; a child grows, a culture develops, a person dreams. In every area of human thought, civilization has evolved a functioning reality, but the universe has suffered no reality to maintain itself unchanged. The glory of man is that he is not bounded by reality. Man travels in fantastic worlds.

[68] Kuhn, *The Structure of Scientific Revolutions*.
[69] J.R.R. Tolkien, "On Fairy Stories," in *The Tolkien Reader*, Ballantine, New York, 1966, p. 55.

# Index

229

*Library of Congress Cataloging in Publication Data*

Rabkin, Eric S
The fantastic in literature.

Includes index.
1. Fantastic literature—History and criticism.
I. Title.
PN56.F34R3    809'.91'5    75-30201
ISBN 0-691-06301-X    (hardcover edn.)
ISBN 0-691-01340-3    (paperback edn.)